THE TOKEN CHARISMATIC

The Gifts of the Spirit and Speaking in Tongues

CONTENTS

CHAPTER 3

MY PERSONAL EXPERIENCE

Miracles are still happening

CHAPTER 4

My friend John MacArthur

A great man, a wonderful friend, but he has missed it on this issue

CHAPTER 5

DEFINING THE NINE GIFTS OF 1 CORINTHIANS 12

Proper Biblical definitions and examples

PROPHECY IN THE NEW TESTAMENT

What actually is Prophecy: How it functions and its purpose

CHAPTER 6

WORD OF KNOWLEDGE AND

WORD OF WISDOM

Supernatural, not natural

CHAPTER 7

LET'S TALK ABOUT TONGUES

Is it a real language or just "Yabba Dabba Doo"

CHAPTER 8

THE GIFT OF INTERPRETATION OF TONGUES

Are there any Biblical examples?

CHAPTER 9

HEALINGS AND MIRACLES

Why did Jesus do miracles?

ALWAYS READ THE PREFACE

PREFACE

The reason I am writing this book is to bring clarity on what has been written and spoken by the Cessationists camp of theology concerning the Gifts of the Holy Spirit and speaking in other tongues. Among them is a personal friend of mine, Dr. John MacArthur, someone with whom I have shared wonderful fellowship, both spiritually in dialogue and casually on the golf course, for over twenty years. And he will continue to be my friend when the dust settles after this book has been printed and read by you. This book is meant to be irenic, not divisive.

Dr. MacArthur called me before this book ever went to print and as we were setting up our next golf date, I told him about this book I was writing in response to his work called "Strange Fire." He said to me, **"Gary, if you think writing this book would hurt our friendship, I want you to know it will not. I appreciate you getting hold of me (I had emailed him to call me) and letting me know. It is "FAIR GAME" (his words) to do so. I have written many books on the things I believe, and you have every right to write what you believe in response to mine."** I appreciate John's attitude towards my work on these subjects.

John and his colleagues have dubbed me "The Token Charismatic" in the group whenever we are together, thus the title of this book. I will quote extensively from not only many of the books John has written-most of them are really well done-but also from CDs John has put out over the years concerning the topic of the Holy Spirit and Charismatics.

You can research and refer to these his books which I will quote from, but the CDs may require a little more work on your part to obtain. However, I will list the title of the message concerning the CDs that I am quoting from, and if you simply call, email, or write GRACE TO YOU (GTY) in Southern California, they will be more than happy to send you the CDs at your request, and I believe at no charge.

The reason I include portions of his teaching sermons on CD in this book is due to the fact that if any of us as preachers are putting out our sermons to the public by way of radio, TV, Internet, MP3, or CD, we should stand behind what we have said just as though it were in print. Because I have followed John's ministry for more than two decades, I have a wide collection of his teachings.

I own his New Testament Commentary series, many of which were sent to me as a gift from John, as well as most of the books he has written on a variety of topics.

They are worth having and reading for yourself. John, as many of you know, has a worldwide teaching ministry and all his teachings are on CD. I own many of these as well. He has said many things against the Gifts of the Spirit, Charismatics, and speaking in tongues, which I will quote from and refute.

In addition, I have been a supporter of Grace To You ministry for most of these years, and in return, GTY sends out free CDs of John's teachings on a regular basis. That is why in this book I will quote from both John's written works and his spoken words on CD. By the way, John has been kind enough over the years to listen to my sermons on CD which I have sent to him, and has always been kind enough to call or write and let me know that he had listened to the message or messages. For that I am eternally grateful. That John would take time to befriend a "Charismatic" has given me a special sense of acceptance, and that he would take the time to listen to my teachings has been a true honor as a "Son in the Faith."

I am very aware of the command which Paul gave to Timothy concerning addressing older men in the church; "Do not rebuke an older man harshly, but exhort him as if he were your father" (1Tim 5:1). I will be respectful of John as a spiritual father to me, and as a man older than I am. As Paul also said to Timothy, "The things you have heard me say in the

8

presence of many witnesses entrust to reliable men who will also be qualified to teach others" (2Tim 2:1-2). John has mentored me for years through his teaching of the Word of God and his friendship. For this I am also eternally grateful.

So you might ask, "Why are you writing a book against your spiritual father?" It is not so much against John as it is against things he has said and is saying. Some of these things are simply inaccurate and need to be corrected. Remember the reason John wrote Strange Fire; he felt someone needed to speak up concerning the abuses and heresies which are being done and said, supposedly in the name of Christ, in the so-called Charismatic community. I also believe that someone needs to bend the steel back to an accurate position concerning Charismatic theology, from which John has bent it too far.

As I said, John is my friend and will still be my friend at the end of all this; we just do not agree on these couple of issues. Unfortunately, these issues carry significant weight in the kingdom of God and for that I reason I do not apologize. I love John and he loves me, but I cannot agree with him on these subjects.

John not only has listened to my sermons and commented on them to me, but he has also read the three other books I have written; Be A Man, The Beauty of a Woman, and Let's Get the Gay Thing Straight. As a pastor of 2,000 plus people myself, I know how busy he is, pastoring 10,000 people. In addition, he is also the president of the Master's college and seminary. For him to take the time to read and listen to my "stuff" has demonstrated his friendship to me at a deeper level. Thank you, John.

What I have written in this book is out of deep love for him as a brother, fellow soldier and minister, as well as a dear friend. I also write this work to help people who have read John's books or have listened to his CDs, to see that NOT ALL Charismatics are missing it. I am only doing what John has taught me to do, speak up against error in the church. I am only going to be addressing the nine Gifts listed in 1 Corinthians 12-14. I will not be including the gifts listed in Romans 12, Ephesians 4, and 1 Peter 4, even though these are Gifts also given by God. But the Gifts given in 1 Corinthians are the most hotly debated in Christian circles today.

Whenever I am referring to the Gifts in 1 Corinthians 12 and 14, I will always capitalize the word "Gifts." When I am speaking about other types of gifts mentioned in the Bible, I will not capitalize them. In addition, whenever I mention any of the nine Gifts, I will also capitalize each of them; i.e. Tongues, Prophecy, Miracles, etc.

Even though at times I can be jocular in my sermons, I am very serious concerning the things I am stating in this book. Yet, at times I may use humor to make a salient point. I do find some things said by those in the opposing camp to be misguided and unfounded and this is what I will point out unequivocally.

Yes, John has been, and is, very valuable to the Christian community concerning many orthodox historical Christian doctrines. Yet, I know that he is not accurate concerning ALL CHARISMATICS being in error, and also concerning what we preach about the Holy Spirit and His gifts, including tongues. John uses *ad hominem* arguments against many of the so-called leading Charismatics. **Webster defines ad hominem as, "To the man; - of an argument directed at one's prejudices rather than one's intellect."** (In practice, it is often resorted to in order to evade the force of an opponent's argument by attacking his character, motives, ability, etc. Thus it seeks to destroy the credibility of his witness without answering his argument).

It is only after expostulating many times in many conversations with John, both in person and on the phone, asking him to please truncate the list of those he includes in his statements as heretical, and even after promising me on more than one occasion that he would be careful about how he says things, he capitulated to his flesh and made many unfortunate comments in his work Strange Fire, which is replete with egregious statements, concerning ALL OF US (Charismatics) in this camp.

John is my friend, but I must share the truth from the OTHER CAMP of what the Holy Spirit is still doing in the Kingdom of God today. I know that you will prayerfully read this book, asking the Lord for understanding. As Paul the Apostle said, "We do not write you anything you cannot read or understand"

(2 Corinthians 1:13).

A soldier in God's army,

Pastor Gary

Chapter 1

ARE YOU SURE?

With so many different denominations within Protestantism, and each holding on to their pet doctrines, trying to understand what we believe about certain Christian theologies can be a difficult endeavor, to say the least.

For example:

    a. What do you believe about the second coming of Christ? Will it happen before the Tribulation, during the Tribulation, or after the Tribulation?

    b. Do you believe there is a Tribulation coming or is this just symbolic language?

    c. What do you believe concerning when a person should be water baptized? Should they be baptized as an infant, or as an adult when they give their life to Christ?

    d. Should they be fully submerged, sprinkled on, or hosed off?

e. Are we to baptize people in Jesus name only, or in the name of the Father, Son, and Holy Spirit?

f. What do you believe about God electing some people for salvation and others for damnation?

g. Or, do you believe in Free Choice, meaning that each person has a say in whether or not they give their life to Christ?

h. And how about speaking in tongues? Is it still for today? Do some people really have this gift or is it just "gibberish" or even demonic?

i. How about the "Gifts of the Holy Spirit?" Do people still have access to them today or were they just for a short period of time in the early church until the completion of the New Testament?

j. Does salvation require faith and works or is it solely by faith?

k. Is the Bible THE Word of God or does it simply contain the words of God?

l. Can people lose their salvation once they are saved, or is it once saved, always saved?

m. Do the bread and wine become the actual body and blood of Christ or are they simply symbolic?

n. Can women preach or pastor in the local church or are they to remain completely silent in the public assembly?

o. What is your stance on people who call
    themselves Christians but profess to be gay?
p. Should Christians worship on Saturday or
    Sunday, or is every day alike?
q. Do you believe in a rapture of the church or just
    His second coming?
r. Can you explain the Trinity and is it found in
    the Bible?
s. Has the church replaced Israel as the elect of
    God or will the Jewish people one day be
    saved?

The list goes on and on...

That is a lot to ponder and figure out. Some people
believe if you don't agree with them on these points
that you may not be saved, or are at the very least a
somewhat deficient Christian.

The answers which many Christians give to these and
a host of other good questions are usually more
subjective than objective. By that I mean they answer
based on what they "feel" rather than on what the
Word of God says. But even then, how do Bible
believing Christians who do look to the Word of God

for their answers, differ on how they interpret the very texts they stand on?

All the questions listed above (and many more) are still hotly debated in Christian circles today. We have divided into groups (denominations) and yet we all feel that we are right and the others are wrong. Theology, instead of bringing us together, has actually caused divisions amongst us. As Paul said to the Corinthians, "there have to be differences among you to show which of you has God's approval" (1 Cor 11:19). Of course, Paul was not giving them a compliment, but rather a rebuke because they weren't in agreement on things.

Indeed, there are theological topics where there is room for opposing ideas, such as Paul stated in Romans 14, things he calls "disputable matters." These are the issues which the great theologian Augustine said "In the essentials, unity, in the non-essentials, liberty, and in all things, charity."

The late Dr. Walter Martin, founder and president of the Christian Research Institute (now headed up by Hank Hanagraf) and the original voice of 'The Bible Answer Man' program once said, "If we are going to hang all the Pentecostal theologians and leaders for insisting on the Gifts of the Spirit, then let's go all the way and hang the reformers too. Calvin, Luther, Zwingli, and Knox, for they insisted on them also"

(Walter Martin ministries; resource catalog, CD entitled 'Gifts of the Holy Spirit' #3022). In this book, I will be dealing specifically with the theologies of the Gifts of the Spirit and speaking in tongues.

As a Pastor, I will be judged more strictly for what I say and teach (James 3:1). The reason is, if I stand up and teach others about Christian doctrine, I should know what I am talking about and believe, and I am also required to live what I preach. We are commanded as leaders to "Study to show ourselves approved unto God, as one who rightly handles the word of truth." (2 Timothy 2:15). So, how can so many good and godly men differ on these things, and who really is right concerning them? We can't all be right, can we? Every true believer has a theology (belief) about them. Whether they can prove it or not is another matter. They may not even know which scriptures to turn to in support of their belief; they just know they believe it.

Some Christians hold to their beliefs because it just seems right or fair. For example, many believe that we have a "Free Choice" in accepting or rejecting salvation once we hear the gospel. The reason they believe this is because it is tough to swallow a belief that says God chooses **SOME** He wants to save, but

ALL the others He simply allows to die in their sins, almost like He loves some people but not others.

Having that "feeling" about God, they choose the doctrine of Free Choice rather than Election. But can they prove it from scripture? And what will they say in response to the scriptures which talk about God's election? Not an easy problem to solve.

On the other hand, others believe in the doctrine of election because their "teachers" have told them "this is what all reformed theologians have taught" and to believe anything else would be against Christian doctrine. So they have to believe it, or else! But does that make them right?
And, by the way, there are scriptures and church traditions that seem to advocate and support all of these theologies.

Yet, we should know why we believe what we believe. We are to give an answer to everyone who asks us for the hope we have (1 Peter 3:15). Yet, if one person asks two different Christians any of these questions, they are likely to get at least three different answers!

But probably the top two topics that have caused (and still cause) the most division and arguments in Christianity today are the issues of the *Gifts of the Holy Spirit* and *speaking in other tongues,* both found in 1 Corinthians 12-14. In this book I will argue for the **continuation** of both spiritual gifts and speaking in other tongues, over against the theological stance that they **ceased** after the completion of scripture or the death of the Apostles. I know that if you have an open mind and carefully search out what I am about to unfold from the scriptures, you too will see that both of these (spiritual gifts and speaking in tongues) are necessary and beneficial to the believer and the body of Christ today.

**Below is a quote from a letter written by John Wesley to Thomas Church in June 1746 in which he states:

Yet I do not know that God hath anyway precluded Himself from thus exerting His sovereign power for working miracles in any kind or degree in any age to the end of the world. I do not recollect any scripture wherein we are taught that miracles were to be confined within the limits either of the apostolic or the Cyprianic age, or of any period of time, longer or shorter, even till the restitution of all things, I have not

*observed, either in Old testament, or the New, any
intimation at all of this kind.*

*St. Paul says, indeed, once, concerning two of the
miraculous gifts of the Spirit (so, I think, that test is
usually understood), 'Whether there be prophecies,
they shall fail; whether there be tongues, they shall
cease.' But he does not say, either that these, or any
other miracles shall cease till faith and hope shall
cease also, till they be swallowed up in the vision of
God, and love be all in all."* (- Tedford, The Letters of
John Wesley, nd. 2:261).

Unfortunately one of the main opponents of these two
doctrines (the Gifts of the Spirit and Tongues) is a dear
friend of mine, Dr. John MacArthur, the voice of the
"Grace to You" radio program and Senior Pastor of
Grace Bible Church in Sun City, California. He
believes that some of the Gifts found in 1 Corinthians
12 have ceased, (thus the name Cessationists), and that
any so-called Gifts today are an aberration of the true
and real Gifts in which the early church operated.

Because I have spent quite a bit of time with Dr.
MacArthur over the last 20 years, and have had many
conversations with him on a variety of subjects, I will
often refer to his statements on CD, his books and
statements made to me in person, to show the

inaccuracies from the Cessationists' camp concerning these two theologies. John is my dear friend, and because of our conversations concerning this particular subject, I thought it only right and fair to write the arguments "for" the doctrine of the Gifts of the Spirit and speaking in tongues, which are still in operation today.

Whenever John and I play golf together (usually a couple of times a year, he living in Southern and I in Northern California), he calls me the "Token Charismatic" in the group. Though we are at polar opposites concerning this subject, we have accepted each other as brothers in Christ. For that I am very grateful. We can agree to disagree. Yet, I do believe his stance, along with those who hold to the same belief, is robbing the church of great blessing. That is why I am writing this book, to help believers know that the power of God and His gifts are still available to them today.

In my conversations with Dr. MacArthur, he has not been able to refute any of my arguments from scripture, nor convince me that I am theologically in error. You, the reader, will have to make up your own mind and prayerfully study and search out the path which you will land on concerning these two vitally important doctrines; Tongues and the Gifts of the Spirit.

As the token Charismatic in the group, I've always been in the minority whenever I am with John and those from the Cessationists' camp. But I know whom I have believed and I am very confident in my stance. I think you too will see that God never meant for His Gifts to be "just for a moment in time," but rather, they were to be the "lifeblood" of the church in ministering to each other and to a lost and dying world.

In fact, on one occasion when we were playing at one of John's Country Clubs, Spanish Hills, we were on the second hole par 5 playing with two of his pastor friends, neither of which came from the Charismatic persuasion. One of them began talking with me about my theology of the Holy Spirit and the gifts. While we waited to hit our approach shots, I began to share with him about what God was doing during our assembly times. As he listened intently, I looked over and noticed that John and the other pastor were also listening. I told them that during our worship times, God will, at times, give me words of knowledge concerning people who are present and often healings take place. This one pastor who had asked me about this said to me, "I've always wanted to know about this. I've been asking God for more in our assembly times. How does it happen?"

I was surprised to hear him make say this right in front of John. I began to tell him that for me, it has required extra time in isolated prayer and fellowship with the Lord, asking Him to use me for His glory. I then told him (knowing that these were John's friends), that you, the pastor, have to step out in faith and make room for the leading of the Holy Spirit and when you believe He is giving you something to share or do, you trust God's leading.

John heard every word I said to those two pastors and he himself never said a word to correct or refute what I had said to them. I am not saying that his silence was agreement, but simply, he believed that what I was telling his friend was either the truth or not. He could not deny my experiences in the gifts and without any scripture to support his belief that they had stopped, he graciously remained silent.

I will not, or ever want to, attack John's character for his belief in this matter. John is a man of God, plain and simple. He is a man of great and godly character and he is my friend. What I do want to do is show where John and others who hold to the Cessationist view are in error. I will not be pedantic about this study, but I will be thorough as I walk you through the scriptures. You will definitely want to have your Bible handy as you read through this book. You may or may not agree with what I say by the time you finish reading it, but you will not be able to deny that the scriptures say what they say. It will be your choice to decide where you land theologically when you are finished.

CHAPTER 2

NOT IN MY CHURCH!

Have you ever experienced a healing touch from God in your physical body?

Or, has anyone ever prayed for you, and what you thought was an impossible situation simply turned around in your favor?

Have you ever prayed for someone else and God miraculously healed them?

Have you ever been in a church service or with some Christian people who believed in the power of God, and suddenly extraordinary things began to happen?

I was raised in a Pentecostal/Charismatic family and I have been in many church services which were downright silly and steeped in Pentecostal culture. Yes, I have seen some things that were quite embarrassing and I personally do not believe they were from God. However, I have also been a Foursquare Pastor (which is a Charismatic/Pentecostal denomination) in Northern California for over 26 years now, and we believe in the Gifts of the Spirit still being alive and available today. I have personally seen and have been a part of God healing people and allowing His gifts to be used in many of our church services as well.

While it is true that many Christians believe God is able to heal and do supernatural things, many do not believe that they happen much today, if at all. But I am here to tell you that He does and He still wants to. I will show from scripture (The Word of God), and also give you historical and personal accounts in the pages which follow, to verify what the Word of God teaches us today concerning God, miracles, healings, and the Gifts of His precious Spirit.

Whether you believe what you are about to read or not will be totally up to you. Even if you end up not believing in these things, again I say, you will not be able to deny them. You will not be able to walk away and say, "The Bible does not say that."

God's Word is clear; He is a supernatural God! He loves to give out **supernatural** gifts to **natural** people like you and me. This was true of the early church and it still applies to us today. Let's look at what was and is and shall continue to be, if we allow it. "Jesus Christ is the same yesterday, today and forever" (Hebrews 13:8).

ACTS 14:8-10

"In Lystra there sat a man crippled in his feet, who was lame from birth and had never walked. He listened to Paul as he was speaking. Paul looked directly at him, saw that he had faith to be healed and called out, "Stand up on your feet!" At that, the man jumped up and began to walk."

Would this ever happen in our churches today? *Could* this ever happen in our churches today? Do the gifts of the Holy Spirit still operate in the Body of Christ like they did in the early church or in the first century? If you listen to many pastors and teachers in our time, the answer would be a resounding "NO!" But are they right? By what authority can they definitively say this? What scriptures do they stand on to make such unwarranted claims? Can you give me one scripture, just one, where the Bible says that the Gifts of Healings would come to a halt in our day? It's time we stop listening to nay-sayers and "examine the scriptures every day to see if what they say is true" (Acts 17:11).

I have attended churches of many different denominations and have seen things from one end of the spectrum of Christianity to the other. I have been in services where, on one hand, if you clapped or raised your hands, you were looked at as though you were causing an unnecessary disturbance or were being 'overly emotional.' On the other hand, I have seen people jump, dance, knock off wigs and speak in what may or may not have been tongues, and everyone acted like this was a perfectly normal happening.

So who is right? I'm not talking about preference or church etiquette. I'm not talking about style or a difference in church cultures. I am talking about, does the Holy Spirit get an opportunity to lead and have a say-so when it comes to the direction our church services take? Usually, the pastor and the leadership team set the direction and the tone in any given church service, and we are the ones who either allow or disallow things to happen in these corporate gatherings. But would we allow what Paul permitted in Acts 14 to ever take place in our times together in the 21st century? More importantly, do we even believe it could take place? Let's take an honest look at scripture and a couple of real life experiences and see what we come up with, shall we?

Let's take a closer look at this story in Acts 14.

Paul and Barnabas were on their first missionary journey, having been sent out from the church they co-pastored in Syrian Antioch, north of Jerusalem. It was a diverse church made up of a sprinkling of Jews and many different Gentiles. Even though the mother church was in Jerusalem (and the lead pastor was none other than the Lord's brother James, along with Peter and John) the church in Antioch was one of the largest, if not the largest of the early churches in the book of Acts. (Acts 19:24-26)

As Paul and Barnabas were commissioned by the Holy Spirit (Acts 13:2) to go on their first missionary journey, they first traveled to Barnabas' hometown on the isle of Cyprus. From there they went on to Pisidian Antioch where they had some success winning people to Jesus, and from there they were off to Iconium. Unfortunately, even though they were winning the lost in this city, they were run out of town. They ended up in nearby Lystra, where the miracle took place concerning the man who had been born crippled, and while listening to Paul preach, had faith to be healed (Acts 14:8-).

Luke records this event for us, and please remember he was a doctor. He reported that the man was crippled, that he was born this way, and that he had never walked, ever. Luke is writing this story to a man named Theophilus, informing him of the power of God, the authority of the name of Jesus, and the importance of faith in God. Only a miracle could have healed this man.

Luke says that as Paul was preaching, he saw that the man had faith to be healed. What exactly did Paul see? Did the man hold up a sign saying, "I have faith to be healed?" Was he wearing a tee shirt or a hat saying this? And what does faith look like on someone's face? How did Paul know the man had faith to be healed? Does faith have a certain appearance to it?

Whatever it was, Paul knew it, and he immediately stopped preaching and told the man to act on his faith, get up and walk.

Let's go a little deeper. What was Paul preaching that enabled this man's faith to rise to such a level that he could be healed? It couldn't have just been the simple gospel of salvation. The gospel does provide an opportunity for salvation as the Spirit of God draws the individual
(John 6:44,65). We all know that salvation is the most important thing (Luke 10:20). But it says "as he listened to Paul, he had faith to be healed." There is no doubt that at least part of what Paul was preaching was the healing power of Jesus Christ through faith in His name. Paul was preaching the "Full Gospel"- Jesus Christ Savior and Healer!

He had to be telling the crowds about the miracles Jesus had done, "How God anointed Jesus of Nazareth with the Holy Spirit and power, and how He went around doing good and healing all who were under the power of the devil, because God was with Him" (Acts 10:38). He also told them all that Jesus began to DO and TEACH (Acts 1:1). He also was telling them that "the reason the Son of God appeared was to destroy the devil's work" (1 John 3:8).

Paul must have told them how "Jesus went throughout Galilee, teaching in their synagogues, preaching the good news of the kingdom, and healing every disease and sickness among the people. News about Him spread all over Syria, and people brought to Him all who were ill with various diseases, those suffering severe pain, the demon possessed, those having seizures, and the paralyzed, and he healed them" (Matthew 4:23-24).

These had to be the things Paul was preaching to the crowds. Just listening to these things now, is enough to lift the faith of anyone. And why would Paul be preaching them if Jesus didn't still do them? By the way, most scholars agree that Timothy, his mother Eunice and his grandmother Lois were in the crowd that day, and this is when Timothy gave his heart to Christ (see Acts 16:1-3).

Later, when Paul was writing his final letter to Timothy he told him, "What you heard from me, keep as the pattern of sound teaching, with faith and love in Christ Jesus" (2 Timothy 1:13). And then in Chapter 2 he says, "You then, my son, be strong in the grace that is in Christ Jesus. And the things you have heard me say in the presence of many witnesses, entrust to reliable men who will also be qualified to teach others" (2 Timothy 2:1-2).

What were the things Timothy had heard from Paul? The full gospel of Jesus Christ. This is what Paul was preaching in Lystra that day which caused the man's faith to rise and become visible on his face. The miracles (faith) and salvation (love) that are in Christ Jesus! When the man in Lystra in Acts 14 heard Paul preaching how Jesus came to heal, deliver, and set people free, faith entered his heart and it showed on his face, and Paul was observant enough to perceive it. Not only was he observant enough to see it, **but he had the sense to get out of the way of his own ego, stop preaching**, look directly at the man, and tell him to get on his feet. "*Paul, the man has never walked*!" Would we ever dare to be so bold?

The simplest cop-out is to say, "This sort of thing doesn't happen anymore." If that is what we believe, we will never tell people that the power of God is still available to them. If we don't tell them, how will they ever receive enough faith to be healed? We not only will never make room for it in our services ("we have to make sure we preach," you know), we also will tell them that the gifts of the Spirit are no longer for today.

For example, Dr. J.Vernon McGee, in his booklet "Speaking in Tongues," says on Page 14, "the sign gifts died out with the apostles." But then on the very next page, 15, he says, "I am willing to grant that on many mission fields today some of these gifts appear." Now wait just a minute; "I object, your Honor!" Either they died out or they didn't! You can't be both pregnant and NOT pregnant at the same time.

No wonder we have such a weak and powerless church today; many pastors do not believe God for the miraculous. And by the way, God loves to be known as the God of the miraculous. It is pastors and Christian leaders who have sold this bill of goods to us. Nowhere in scripture does it say that the Gifts of the Spirit would ever stop in our age. Nowhere! Unfortunately, it is men like my good friend John MacArthur and others who have national and international platforms who are teaching this kind of doctrine. John and I have had many conversations on this and similar doctrines and he has yet to prove his point.

Now, I love John, and as I have already stated, we have been good friends for over 20 years, but I could not disagree with him more on this subject. On many things, we do agree. We have shared wonderful fellowship throughout the years and I thoroughly enjoy his company. I know his wife Pat, and all four children including his two sons, Matt and Mark with whom I have also played golf with quite a few times. By the way, his wife, Pat, used to attend a Foursquare church! John once jokingly said, "I'm still trying to get her to buy my books." However, my good friend John is not correct in his theology when it comes to this subject of the gifts. I will share more about that as we move ahead in this book.

Let me give you another example from the ministry of Jesus concerning what took place when men like Jesus, Peter, and Paul were following the leading of the Holy Spirit whenever they were assembled in church.

In Luke 13, Jesus was teaching in the local synagogue, and a woman was there who had been crippled for 18 years. Now please understand, Jesus was the master teacher. It just didn't get any better than having Jesus in your pulpit. As Jesus was waxing eloquent, he noticed this woman (who was probably seated near the back of the church) who had arrived late so as not to be noticed, sitting in what was her usual seat; you know, the same chair that we always go and sit in every Sunday. The one where you might "get in the flesh" if someone else were sitting in it. I can just see her with dark shades on and a bandana wrapped tightly around her head. As she assumed her same seat in the church, she was probably enjoying this new teacher, Jesus. He was a breath of fresh air, compared to all the other stale rabbis who usually spoke on the Sabbath.

She never had in mind or even dreamed that the guest speaker that day, as good as he was, would embarrass her by calling her forward in front of everyone. I mean, all the other speakers had only wanted to have their turn to teach. They weren't so concerned with the real life issues most of the people were struggling with. By golly, they had a message to preach and only so many minutes to preach it because the people's attention span isn't that long and people have places to go, things to do, and people to see. Never had anyone cared about her condition before. Surely this itinerant preacher wouldn't pay her any mind. Boy, was she in for a surprise.

In the middle of His sermon (just like Paul in Acts 14), Jesus stops. He looks directly at her, and calls her forward, in front of everyone. Talk about the ultimate embarrassment. She has to come from the back of the church and shuffle her way down the aisle while everyone is looking at her. I can just see her saying, "Excuse me. Pardon me. I'm so sorry," as she makes her way to the front. It must have seemed like a mile down to the altar.

But wait a minute. Did Jesus just stop his sermon? The master teacher of all time? If she ever needed to hear another sermon, it was from this guy. He spoke as one with authority. He made things easy to understand. He used great illustrations to help the people relate to what He was saying. But it wasn't another sermon she needed. If she did, Jesus would have kept on teaching. He was probably going to get an honorarium. They were paying Him to teach, not take a liberty because "The Holy Ghost told him to." But Jesus saw her real need and it wasn't another sermon, it was a touch from the Holy Spirit by someone who had "the goods" who could relieve her of this bondage which had been placed on her by the devil himself.

Again, Luke was a doctor. His diagnosis wasn't that she had scoliosis. She didn't have a blown disk from trying to lift something too heavy. Her L4 and L5 in her lower back weren't out from sleeping on the wrong mattress. She didn't have lower back pain from a rear-end car collision. It wasn't sore and tired muscles from working in the garden too long the day before.

Jesus said that the devil had done this to her! It was a spiritual condition with a physical manifestation. Jesus was discerning the spirit who was causing the condition.

Another teaching from the Word of God would not have been enough to heal this woman. And today, in our churches, it's not just more teaching that people need, as important as it is; they need the raw power of God to "heal all that are oppressed of the devil."

But if we are being told this is no longer available to us, what hope do people have? More teaching is good, but remember, Paul said, "knowledge puffs up" (1 Corinthians 8:1). Teach we must! But we also need to allow the Holy Spirit to have His way in our assemblies. We have marginalized Him to the fringes. We have cut our services short otherwise the people won't come, so we are told. We have drive-through gatherings where we sing a song or two, have some creative video announcements, an offering, and then a short homily to appease the people so they will keep coming to our churches. But where is the power of God?

Let me ask a question to those of you who are pastors; what would the Lord, the Spirit, say about our gatherings each week? What if we asked Him what

He wanted to do on this particular Sunday? Would you even consider foregoing your eloquent message to allow a ministry time led by the Holy Spirit under your direct approval and guidance?

To those of you who may be pastors, the Holy Spirit cannot do what He wants in your church assembly unless you allow Him to do so. What if the Holy Spirit leads you, the leader, to just have a time of worship and song, and then directs you to have the people pray for one another for the next 30 minutes? I know you would probably be totally uncomfortable with the "lack of control" you might feel, but once you realize that God is leading you, you will see how freeing this really can be.

Now, let's be clear; I am NOT talking about every week. We know that we as pastors are called to teach and preach God's word. We must "give ourselves to the (public) reading of scripture; to preaching and to teaching" (1 Timothy 4:13). I am a Bible teacher myself - each and every week of my life. I can count on one hand the times in 26 years of preaching that "not preaching" has taken place. But I wonder if there may have been more times when the Spirit of God wanted to do something else that day. I'm sure there were.

So what is my point here? That Jesus and Paul actually stopped their teaching and preaching to minister to the deeper and more immediate needs of people in their congregation. Paul's preaching of Jesus as the healer enabled a man to believe with his heart, not only that Jesus is Lord, but that Jesus wants to heal you. It wasn't Paul's faith that healed him; it was the man's faith. Paul simply was humble enough to stop and let him be healed!

Jesus on the other hand, saw a deeper need than just another "Awesome message, Pastor!" He discerned the devil's work in the woman's life and had a "Charismatic moment." He allowed the Holy Spirit to do His thing. This was real church!

Let me give you some examples when the Spirit of God was allowed to have His way in our public gathering, and I was still able to preach in that service.

CHAPTER 3

My personal experiences with the Gifts of the Spirit

"There is someone in this room who is deaf in your right ear. Come forward now, please. God wants to heal you." This was during one of our Sunday morning worship services, and there were three or four other people who had already come forward with conditions which I had also called out and they were waiting to be prayed for. The man working our sound system that morning came from behind the soundboard and starting walking towards the front of the church. As he came up behind the other people who were standing there waiting for me to pray for them, he lifted his hands and bowed his head with eyes closed, anticipating me to touch him and pray for him.

In his own words later he said, "I had difficulty hearing tones and sounds out of that ear but as Pastor Gary started walking closer, all of a sudden I could literally hear his footsteps coming towards me even though he was walking on the carpet. Instantly I could hear perfectly out of that ear." This man has since become my dear friend. His name is Charles Eric Castenada. That was 18 years ago and today he can still hear perfectly out of that ear.

Two gifts of the Spirit were in operation at that moment; the Word of Knowledge and the Gift of Healing. This same type of event has happened many times in our church services over the 22 years I have been the Senior Pastor of Faith Fellowship Worship Center in San Leandro, a city about 15 miles south of where I was raised in Oakland, California. Not only has God used me to operate in these gifts in my own life, but I also have read about them in God's Word the Bible. I have personally attended other services where men of God have operated in this same type of gifting and anointing. In addition, many men and women of God down through the centuries have also operated in these Gifts since the days of the Apostles and have ministered to literally thousands of people, both here in America and on foreign soil. And this is still happening today.

A month or so after Eric's healing in his ear, again during one of our Sunday morning worship services, we were singing and ministering to the Lord, and I sensed the Spirit of God saying to me that there was someone in the room who had severe pain on the side of their head (there were about 300 people there and we were running four services on Sundays with a total of about 1,100 people). When I called it out to our congregation I thought to myself, "Lord, that could be any number of people in our church." I happened to be holding the right side of my head as I was calling out this condition, and the Lord spoke to my heart and

said, "Name the side of your head you are touching."
So I said, "OK, it is the right side of your head where
the pain is coming from." Instantly a man came out of
his seat and started walking towards the front, crying
as he approached the altar. This man had been coming
to our church for just a short time and had recently
accepted Jesus as his Lord and Savior.

As he approached, I said to him, "Richard, I don't
know why you have come forward but God wants to
heal you." As he held his head in his hands, crying, I
reached out my hand to pray for him but I never got to
touch him because instantly he felt power go through
him and he said he was healed. All the pain left him
immediately. He is still healed today, just like Charles
Castenada. His name is Richard Guest. Let me tell
you his story as he told it to me.

Richard is an electrician and he was working at Alta
Bates hospital in Berkeley California when one day as
he was working, he fell 15 feet through the 2nd floor
ceiling and landed on an operating table on his right
side, doing soft tissue damage to his head and breaking
a few of his ribs. He said he actually "straight-lined"
(died) for 45 seconds. After the accident he was put
on medications for constant migraines, but the
medicine made him incredibly moody. We knew him
as a moody type guy but had no idea why, that is until
he was healed and he told us his story. He was on a

mood altering drug for close to five years when he started going to our church and gave his life to Christ. That is when the Lord gave me a Word of Knowledge about someone with pain in the right side of their head. He said that when he came forward to be prayed for, he instantly felt the power of God touch him and to this day, 18 years later, he is still healed!

These "Gifts of the Spirit" are still in operation today, and they will be until Jesus comes again. We the church, the people of God, have been given the Holy Spirit to be His witnesses to a lost and dying world. But remember what Jesus said, "You shall receive POWER, when the Holy Spirit comes upon you." These gifts were given, not so we could show off, or boast that "by our own power and godliness" (Acts 3:12) these people get healed. May it never be! But rather, that we might minister to one another and to a lost, sick, and sin-filled world. "But you shall receive power when the Holy Spirit comes upon you."

An International Evangelist friend of mine, Mario Murillo, who is a native of the Bay Area where I am from (he now lives in Reno Nevada), and someone who discipled me in my early years in the ministry, is well known by many top evangelical leaders. Pastors like Jack Hayford and Tommy Barnett, both have had him speak in their pulpits dozens of times. Mario reports the following two miraculous healings which took place in his crusades. In his own words he states:

"A meeting in Baltimore produced one of the most staggering healings we had ever seen. As I sat in the lobby of the hotel, I saw a violent vision. The Spirit of God revealed a man being robbed and stabbed and left for dead. God said, 'When you stand to speak, describe this vision and the man will be healed.' The man was Warren Rogers. He delivered bread in the ghetto. He was robbed, stabbed, and then had his legs cruelly broken by his assailants. He lost the use of his legs. John Hopkins University pricked his legs over 1,000 times trying to find a live nerve. He became a slap walker in a body brace. When he heard me describe his condition in the auditorium that night, he screamed and tried to walk. To his amazement, he could run! His miracle shook the legal and medical world when he gave back a fortune he won for being disabled so that his miracle would be documented in the courts."

The second testimony is equally astounding. Again, Mario's own words:

"Howard Kratzer was on a waiting list for a heart transplant. When it became clear that he would likely die before receiving one, he moved to Phoenix to spend his last days with his grandchildren.

While in Phoenix, he became an Elder at Phoenix First Assembly of God, under Pastor Tommy Barnett. His physical condition deteriorated to the point that he

*was now taking the highest dosage of nitroglycerin in
Arizona history. His doctor told him that the bottom
half of his heart was dead.*

*In August of 1993, Howard attended our healing rally
at Phoenix First Assembly. I looked to my right and
saw a man's face that made every other face in the
room grow dim. I found myself saying, 'You have a
heart condition. Raise your hands to God.'*

*I didn't know that his Doctor had solemnly warned
him to never raise his hands above his ears or he
would have a massive heart attack. Howard obeyed
my words and raised his hands high. Instead of a
heart attack, he received a miracle! He returned to the
doctor for more tests and the doctor told him, 'You do
not have the same heart.' 24 years later, Howard
enjoys perfect health."*

Mario is a close personal friend. I have stood on the
platform with him and have even led worship at his
crusades and have witnessed him operate in the Word
of Knowledge and Gifts of Healings. Not all are as
dramatic as these, but some are. I am not one to easily
believe Charismatic "stuff," but I know Mario
personally

These are true, documented healings which have been
verified. I could give you hundreds more, yes,
thousands more. But what are you going to do with
them? Are you going to deny them? And if so, why?
But if they are real, does this not give credence and
validity to the gifts still being in operation, just like the

Bible promises? Or, will you simply discount them because you begin with the belief that you don't believe they are still for today? It's now your call.

What will you do when you, or someone you love gets sick or contracts a disease? You are going to pray and ask God to heal them. To have mercy on them. To shower them with grace and compassion and deliver them. Right? But what if you believe that God doesn't heal anymore?

What if you believe that your prayers aren't "strong enough." Or maybe you think your life isn't holy enough? I mean we all know how sinful we can be. But what if I told you, and you believed me, that God the Holy Spirit loves to give out Gifts to the Body of Christ, and those Gifts are still available today? You would run to the nearest "faith-healer" in hopes that God will use this person and the Gifts God provides to do a miracle. The problem is, we have been told by so many Christian leaders that the Gifts of the Spirit are not for today. We have been told that God stopped giving out His Gifts when the last Apostle died. That there are no individuals who actually have the true Gifts that God originally gave to the church in Corinth, and that, pretty much, you are "outta luck buddy, you're going to die!"

I want to be fair and clear about something first. Many of the teachers and preachers who speak AGAINST any modern day Christians operating in the gifts of the

Spirit would never deny that God can and does heal from time to time if He wants to. I mean, He is God, right? They say (and I agree) that God is sovereign and He can do what He wants, when He wants, how He wants, to whomever He wants. Some of them even teach the principle found in the epistle of James which says, "Is anyone of you sick? He should call the elders of the church to pray over him and anoint him with oil in the name of the Lord. And the prayer offered in faith will make the sick person well; the Lord will raise him up" (James 5:14). Most of them agree with this passage in James (though not all). Many of these same preachers may also lay hands on people and ask the Lord to heal them, hoping that He will. But what they will NOT teach and do not believe is any believer today can have any of the nine Gifts found in 1 Corinthians 12.

In their book "The Charismatic Century," written by Dr. Jack Hayford and Dr. David Moore, they name many people who in the last 100 years have operated in the Gifts of the Spirit, most notably the Gifts of Healings. Six people in particular, four men and two women, have been researched, and documented healings have been confirmed as a result. These six people are Oral Roberts, A.A. Allan, William Brannon, Aimee Semple McPherson, Benny Hinn, and Kathryn Kulhman. Dr. David Moore is a Pentecostal historian and has researched these findings very carefully. For example, he reports that William

46

Brannon saw over 37,000 people healed in his crusades (1). You are either going to have to accept what he says as true or call him a liar or say that he is badly mistaken. You will have to decide. Dr. Moore and Dr. Hayford have both been Foursquare Pastors and are friends of mine.

Please don't miss this next point: If you do not believe in the Gifts of the Spirit, you will never teach them, and if you don't teach them, you will never make room for them in your services. If you never make room for them in your services they will never happen. This, by the way, will only further cement your belief that they are not for today.

Stop and think that through.

But what if the Holy Spirit WANTS His Gifts to operate in and through us? What if we let the Holy Spirit lead us in our services and our lives? What if, since the Bible doesn't say the Gifts would cease, (in fact it says the opposite, which I will show you), you learned that not only are they still available for the body of Christ today, but that God wanted to use you to operate in them? Didn't Paul say to the church and not to just the apostles, "To eagerly desire spiritual gifts"...? (1 Corinthians 14:1).

This was not to the apostles that he was writing, but rather to a very carnal, disorganized group of believers who were divisive about everything!

What if I walk you through the scriptures and show you that the Gifts were never meant to be "taken back" or "removed" by God. Nor were they meant to come to an end in this age. What if I told you, not that you have been lied to (that would be judging someone's motivation), but rather that Cessationists were mistaken, or that they were deficient in their theology and had absolutely no scriptural support. None!

I will also show you why their arguments are specious and unwarranted and why their theologies on the Gifts of the Spirit and speaking in other languages is hurting the body of Christ and keeping many from being encouraged, used, healed, and blessed. By "them" I mean people, Christians, leaders even, who have a platform to speak, and even though they may be accurate on some Christian doctrines, when it comes to the Holy Spirit and His Gifts, they are DEAD WRONG! Will you believe the Gifts are for today and that they have always operated in the body of Christ if I can show you biblically and historically, as well as from personal experience? Your answer to these questions has huge implications.

THE IMPLICATIONS OF YOUR ANSWERS

Should you choose NOT to believe these historical and verifiable accounts, you will never be open to the miraculous power of God to do great and mighty things in your world. You might respond by saying "God is able to do them if he wants because he is God, but I don't believe he uses people to do them." To that statement I would say "Why not?" Why wouldn't God use people? He has always used people. Ordinary people. He uses people to preach His gospel. Remember, He commands us to "show forth the praiseworthy deeds of our God" (Psalms 78:4).

Jesus said to "go into all the world and preach the gospel, making disciples of all nations, teaching them to obey EVERYTHING I have commanded you" (Matt 28:19-20). What did Jesus command them to do? "Go, I am sending you out like lambs among the wolves" (Luke 10:3). "Heal the sick who are there and tell them, the kingdom of God is near you" (Luke 10:9). God does the healing but He loves to use people. Jesus was commanding people to do these things. By the way, when Jesus gave these commands as recorded in Luke's gospel, He wasn't just sending out the twelve; He was sending out seventy different disciples!

God loves to use people to do His works. He only "can't" if you don't believe He will. But what do you base that belief on? What scriptures do you have to support such a deficient theology? Why wouldn't God use people? We are His hands, His mouth, His servants. Of course He will use us – who else would He use? When Peter prayed in Acts 4:29-30, he said, "Now, Lord, consider their threats and ENABLE YOUR SERVANTS to speak your word with great boldness. Stretch out your hand to heal and perform miraculous signs and wonders through the name of your holy servant Jesus." Did you get that? Enable Your Servants! In fact, in answer to Peter's prayer, in the very next chapter, many were healed just by Peter's shadow passing over them (Acts 5:12-16).

Now you might argue, "Yes, but that was the Apostle Peter." Yes, but the point is, God has always used people to do His work. Even Paul said later to the Corinthian church, "We are therefore Christ's ambassadors, as though God were making his appeal THROUGH US" (2 Corinthians 5:20).

Did you get that? Through us! So if God can, by a sovereign act of His grace, heal people, why is it so hard to fathom that He still uses people like you and me - the church body- to do this? If you say "Because I don't believe the people who say they can do these things are telling the truth," or "Because only a few

50

people in history have done so." Now you are arguing from experience and not from scripture. You are arguing that since the gifts haven't been prolific in church history, then that must mean they stopped. Please remember, that is not an argument based on any scriptures. It is simply a statement you are making from "so-called" history.

As I mentioned earlier in Dr. David Moore and Jack Hayford's book, the "Charismatic Century," they state that many thousands of healings took place which are verified in history. The founder of the Foursquare church, a woman by the name of Aimee Semple McPherson, is recorded to have had thousands of people healed in her crusades and church services. Let me tell you another one that a rancher friend of mine told me about on a hunting trip we went on in Oregon.

The ranchers name is John Justeson. My son and I have hunted on his ranch in North-Eastern Oregon a number of times and over the years he has told me the same story twice. The reason I had him tell me the story twice is because I wanted to get the details exactly right so you would hear it right from the family in which the miracle occurred. John told me that when his father was a young boy (his dad is still alive at the time of this writing, age 90), he became very sick. John's grandmother (his dad's mother) took him from Oregon all the way to Los Angeles to attend an Aimee

Semple McPherson crusade at her 5,000 seat auditorium called Angeles Temple. The grandmother had heard of Aimee's ministry and desperately wanted her son to be healed. She made the long drive with her sickly child in the car and when she got to L.A. Aimee prayed for him and he was completely healed. Did I mention he is still alive at 90? By the way, Aimee had the Gift of Healing and multiple thousands were healed.

Again I state, if you choose not to believe these accounts, the Gifts never will operate in your life or in the life of your church. You might ask, "Why isn't everyone healed or why don't people with this so-called gift go and empty the hospitals?" If they could, they would. What Christian man or woman doesn't want to see people who are suffering or who are dying too young, healed? We all would love to do this, or at least see it. But the very question shows ignorance of how the Gifts of Healings operate.

Remember, the Holy Spirit gives the Gifts as He chooses and the Gift only works when He says it will work. If you ever read the biography or autobiography of the people who have operated in this Gift, from Oral Roberts, to Aimee, to Kathryn Kulhman, to Benny Hinn, they all say the same thing, "I can't heal anyone. I am totally dependent on the Holy Spirit. If He doesn't heal, no one will be healed." Kathryn

Kulhman would say that every time she went on stage to preach and minister, she would die a thousand deaths, pleading with the Holy Spirit to come and do His sovereign work.

But is that any different from Peter praying in Acts 4:29-30, "Now Lord, consider their threats and enable your servants to speak your word with great boldness. Stretch out your hand to heal and perform miraculous signs and wonders through the name of your holy servant Jesus." Why would Peter plead with the Lord like that if he could simply operate in those Gifts anytime he wanted? The reason he prayed like that is because, like us, he was totally dependent on God.

Are you getting it? God gives the Gifts to whom He wants. God wants to use people who believe and are willing to be used. The Gifts operate when He, God, says they will. And again I say, the implications of whether or not you believe in the Gifts are enormous. You either believe I am lying to you about Charles and Richard, the two guys I mentioned at the start, or that I'm mistaken, or that maybe it does happen, albeit seldom. But let me ask you: Isn't seldom better than never? And what if the Gifts only operated "seldom" because of us and not because of God?

Remember what happened to Jesus when he arrived in his own hometown? Mark said, "HE COULD NOT DO ANY MIRACLES THERE, except lay his hands on a few sick people and heal them. And he was amazed at their LACK OF FAITH" (Mark 6:5). In other words, they said, "God can't use you, Jesus. You are one of us. We know where you live. Our kids went to school with you. We have BBQ's with your mom Mary and your dad Joseph. You might be a prophet to others, but you will always be "Bubba to us."

Let us not fall into this same category of people who become so accustomed to church services that we forget part of the reason we are even there; to minister to one another in the name of Jesus.

CHAPTER 4

My friend Dr. John MacArthur

"Hello, is Dr. MacArthur in?" I said. "He's not in right now but this is his secretary, Pat. How may I help you," she said. "My name is Gary Mortara, and I am a Foursquare Pastor from the Bay Area of Northern California and I follow John's ministry. I know he is Scottish so I figure he must play golf, and I was wondering if there might be a time when I can come down and join him for a round of golf," I said. "Oh, let me take your name and number and I will get back to you after I talk to John," she said. So, she took down my phone number and promised to call me back.

A couple of weeks later, another assistant pastor called me back informing me that John pastors 10,000 people and doesn't have time to play golf with other people. I said to him, "Thank you for returning my call, but I know that sometimes as golfers we may only have three of us who can play at any given time and I would fly down on my own dime and pay my own way to join him." He said, "I will ask him again and get back to you." I said "OK," and thanked him.

About a week later he did call back and said John would like me to come down and join him. He gave me two dates to choose from, so I picked one, and that began what has now been over a 20 year friendship between John MacArthur and me.

I have played with Dr. MacArthur almost every year in the annual Master's college golf tournament down in Southern California and have become friends with many of his colleagues and family members. We have enjoyed sweet fellowship for all these many years, and still do, and I have even been dubbed the "Token Charismatic" in the group. We have had many theological discussions about a variety of topics and theologies.

I consider John a friend and I know he considers me one as well. I have flown down to L.A. on a number of occasions just to play golf with him at both of his country clubs, Valencia and Spanish Hills. He has always treated me like a son and we have talked on the phone on a number of occasions. I even had him come up and play golf in the Bay Area with me. John MacArthur is my friend.

It was with great sadness that I learned John was not only writing a book, but he was also having a conference with the same title, "Strange Fire," speaking aggressively against all Charismatics, of which, there is no doubt, I am one. I agree with John on some of his points concerning men and women who have greatly abused gullible people in the kingdom of God with their spiritual weirdness and charades, acting and speaking as though it were the Spirit of God, and it was not.

But, conversely, I have personally operated in the Gifts of the Holy Spirit and have watched genuine moves of the Holy Spirit through other wonderful churches and men and women of God. However, those are experiences and observations. Like you, I want to know what the Bible says about these kinds of things. Are they for today? If the Gifts are still available, who has access to them? How does one operate in them? Are they for everyone? How can there be so much confusion over them if they really are from God? I will answer these and many more questions for you from the Word of God.

I have been in and around many types of churches, many of them Charismatic. I have seen people run down the aisles, jump over pews, knock wigs off, and push people backwards 10 feet or more until they fell down, and they have called it the "power of God." I have also heard messages in tongues without any interpretation following. I have heard "personal prophecies" given to people which weren't even close to being from God. I could go on and on. On these issues I totally agree with my friend John MacArthur. However, he continuously lumps ALL Charismatics in this group of "spiritual silliness" as though that is how ALL Charismatics act and conduct services, and it is not!

In fact, John said to me, walking from the 9th green to the 10th tee at Valencia country club, that he knows I am not that kind of pastor, that I truly love the people God has given me to pastor (over 2,000), and that I teach the Word of God with care, accuracy, and passion. He apologized to me that he had painted with such a broad brush.

In this book I will share more conversations with you that John and I have had, and you are more than welcome to call or write and ask him about them. Again I state, John is my friend, and most of us, even Charismatics, know John to be a wonderfully gifted Bible teacher and student. Most of us use his New Testament commentary series on a regular basis (at least on most issues). He has been a great pastor at Grace Community church and his voice is heard around the world on his radio program "Grace to You." However, that doesn't mean he is right on everything!

I too have a degree in biblical studies and have been on KTLN Television for over 10 years. I am on radio daily right after John MacArthur throughout the Bay Area and I have an audience of hundreds of thousands of people! But that doesn't make me right about everything either. Theology is theology. The study about God from His Word as it is correctly divided or handled (2 Tim 2:15). But what do you do when you have men of great minds who are both saved and love Jesus and serve His people and yet they completely disagree?

For example, John MacArthur and Pastor Jack Hayford from Church on the Way in Van Nuys California have been close friends and fellow soldiers in the ministry for many years. They have shared lunches together and have spoken at each other's churches and conferences. They are both highly esteemed in the Christian community and greatly sought after as speakers in Christian circles. Yet, they are at polar opposites when it comes to the Holy Spirit and His workings.

Oh yes, they agree on the person of the Holy Spirit. They agree on the functions Jesus said the Spirit would operate in concerning teaching, reminding, comforting and so forth. But when it comes to speaking in Tongues and the Gifts being in operation, they couldn't disagree more. How can two respected and knowledgeable Christian leaders be at polar opposites concerning the working of the Holy Spirit and His Gifts through and for the body of Christ today?

John once said to me, "Gary, you form your theology of the gifts of the Spirit from your experience," to which I responded, "And John, you form your doctrine of the Spirit's working from your LACK of experience." In other words, John was saying that my theology of the gifts of the Spirit comes from my experience of speaking in tongues and from having operated in His gifts, not only in my personal life, but also from reading about them in the lives of many Christian leaders in past centuries, and through contemporary Christians who operate in them today.

I told John, "Because you have NEVER operated in the gifts, based on a theology that the gifts of the Spirit don't function in the church today, you are convinced that they don't." However, let me remind ALL OF US that the burden of proof is on the non-charismatics! In other words, the Bible doesn't say the gifts would end in the church; John does! But he gives no biblical proof whatsoever, none.

In addition, if any of the Gifts of the Spirit have ever operated in any believers after the Apostles, the case is closed; they still operate, at least in those who believe they do. If people who were not apostles from time to time operated in Gifts of Healings, Miracles, Prophecy, etc. or did so after the Apostles had died, then that must mean those Gifts are still available.

Now at this point you might ask, "What about all the phony guys on TV and the people who have supposedly been healed but on further investigation were actually not?" Yes, what about them? No one should follow or pay any attention to so called "faith healers" who are deceiving people and stealing money from gullible Christians. The Bible is replete with warnings against false teachers and false prophets. We should "test all things and hold on to the good" 1 Thess 5:21.

People do all kinds of weird stuff in the name of Jesus, which brings shame on both the body of Christ and Christ Himself. Even Paul said that "Some preach Christ out of envy and rivalry and others out of goodwill. The latter do so in love knowing that I am put here for the defense of the gospel. The former preach Christ out of selfish ambition, not sincerely..." (Phil 1:15-17).

In other words, we are to be wise about who is doing and saying what for the kingdom of God. There have always been false teachers and heretical teachings. But that does not mean that everyone with whom you disagree is a false teacher.

This is why on many points I agree with John. There are charlatans out there. There are others who are teaching errant doctrine and hyper-faith theologies, and "name it and claim it" heresies. I don't agree with these either. However, let's not throw out the proverbial baby with the bathwater. Just because there are false teachers and false doctrines doesn't mean that every Charismatic Christian is included. I shared this with John in one of our times together and he agreed, and said to me, "I know you are not that kind of pastor and that you teach the Word of God accurately."

Way back in the 1980's when Jim Bakker and Jimmy Swaggert fell into sin, society in general said that ALL Christians can't be trusted. But that didn't mean they were right, and it surely wasn't appreciated by us who were trying to live right for Jesus. Guilt by association is never a fun or fair thing for anyone. And even though I do believe in the Gifts of the Holy Spirit today, that doesn't mean I teach false doctrines and heretical theologies.

Back in the 80's when these two "giants" fell, we all wanted to stand up and say "Hey, I'm not one of those guys." But it was too late. We all were included in the scandal. Or like the Catholic Church today. Because of all the scandals around the sexual abuse of children by priests and what seems to be a cover-up by the church leadership, people have disengaged from "organized religion." They are "forsaking the assembling of ourselves together" (Hebrews 10:25) as though all connected to this system are guilty as charged. But in reality, there are many devout people in the Catholic Church who love the Lord and had nothing to do with these scandals.

By the way, Charismatics have evangelized many parts of the world for Jesus Christ, and not with errant doctrine. They have prayed for many sick people who were and still are healed.

They have prophesied with a New Testament understanding of prophecy over many people who have been encouraged and blessed and comforted and strengthened in their faith. Charismatics have opened Bible colleges and orphanages, as well as shelters for men and women. They have given aid to the poor and to destitute people groups. They have given their lives on the mission fields and have forsaken all to follow Jesus.

Most of us pastors, who may not be "Super-Mega Church" pastors, preach Jesus Christ crucified, risen, and coming again. We teach the Word of God line upon line. We only want God to be glorified, and we teach our people to stay away from phony and weird stuff that comes blowing through the church. We also teach them to be wise and careful concerning teachings that come from "cunning and crafty men in their deceitful scheming" (Ephesians 4:14).

We Charismatics believe Jesus was God before the manger, was born of a virgin, lived a sinless life, shed His blood on the cross for the sins of the world, died on the cross, and was buried. Then God raised Him from the dead, and He was seen by over 500 witnesses. We believe He ascended to the right hand of God, and that all authority in heaven and earth has been given to

Him. We believe Jesus Is Lord! We also believe
Jesus is coming back one day. And after the final
enemy, death, is destroyed, He shall then hand the
kingdom back to God the Father. This is what we
believe from God's Word and this is what we teach.

In addition, we believe in the present day working and
operation of the Holy Spirit in both sanctification and
in power. Many Charismatic pastors have a better
argument from scripture, and also proof from
EXPERIENCE than non-charismatics do. We believe
the words of Jesus when He said, "You shall do greater
things than I do because I go to the Father" (John
14:12). And again when Jesus said to "stay in
Jerusalem until you receive the Gift my Father
promised" (Acts 1:4). Then in verse 8 of that same
chapter He said, "But you will receive power when the
Holy Spirit comes on you"....

What would that power be for? Just boldness? No,
not just boldness, but Gifts also for the Body of Christ
as listed in 1 Corinthians 12. All 9 of them are "gifts
given by the Holy Spirit as he wills" (1 Cor 12:11).
Why would the Spirit give them to just carnal average
people in the church to use only in the first century?
That makes no sense at all. Paul wasn't writing to
Apostles in the church. He was writing to the church.
"And eagerly desire spiritual gifts" he said to all of
them. And he did not say, "and oh, these are just for a
few years and then they will all be gone."

What Paul was saying was they needed to be mature concerning the operation of the Gifts in the local assembly. But the Corinthians had turned it into a Charismatic circus. But wait; they had turned everything into a circus. Favorite leaders. Sexual sin. Lawsuits. Marriage and sex in marriage. Food offered to idols. The Lord's table at communion. The doctrine of the resurrection, and the Gifts of the Spirit. This was a dysfunctional church at best. But Paul didn't say to do away with the Gifts, but rather, "Therefore my brothers, be eager to prophesy and DO NOT forbid speaking in tongues. But let's do everything decently and in order" (1 Cor 14:39-40).

If you have ever read John MacArthur's commentary on 1 Corinthians 14, and have really taken an honest look at his arguments, you would have to agree that his interpretations of this passage, and many others like it, are weak at best. Listen to his language in that chapter. He uses terms like, "probably," "most likely," or "I think," or "I believe," in his attempt to alter the meaning of what Paul is really and clearly saying. I have to say that when I read his commentary on this portion of scripture, it is very disappointing to see how John interprets what is written.

He does this whenever it comes to the Gifts of the Spirit or things of this nature. For example, in his commentary on the Epistle of James concerning people who are sick, James the Lord's brother says to "call the Elders of the church and let them pray over the sick, anointing them with oil in the name of the Lord (Jesus); and the prayer offered in faith will restore (heal) the one who is sick and the Lord will raise him up."

However, listen to what John states in his commentary on this passage:

"Here is the most misunderstood and disputed portion of this passage. At first glance it appears to be teaching that sick believers can expect physical healing through the prayers of the elders. But such an interpretation is out of harmony with the context." John at this point in his commentary is going to change the very meaning of what James is saying and what has been the interpretation since James wrote it. John continues, "James moves beyond the suffering believers of the previous point to address specifically those who have become weak by that suffering. The weak are those who have been defeated in the spiritual battle, who have lost the ability to endure their suffering." In other words, John is saying that James doesn't mean what we think he means, but rather anyone who is "weak" spiritually, should call for the elders of the church who should then come and 'rub' oil on them (?) and then the Lord will raise them up.

I simply cannot agree with John here.

Dr. Richard Mayhue, who is a very close companion of John's and an associate pastor at Grace church where John pastors, and was also the Dean of Students at the Master's College, writes in his book "The Healing Promise," page 119, that he disagrees with John's interpretation of this portion of the book of James. He says, *"Some have suggested that James 5:14-15 does not deal with the physical at all, but rather with emotional or spiritual distress. However, when you consider 1) the very normal use of* **asthenia** *in the gospels and Acts, 2) the fact that* **kamno** *refers to serious physical illness, and 3) the illustration of Elijah in James 5:17-18, which unquestionably establishes the problem as physical chastisement, then the suggestion that James 5 doesn't deal with the physical is less compelling."*

Please understand, that not even John's faculty totally agrees with John on how he interprets healing in the Word of God. What does that say about how John approaches this subject? He has a pre-determined view in mind and he is not going to let anyone or anything stand in his way, even if they come from his own camp. That is very unfortunate, to say the least.

The reason John does this is due to the fact that he begins with a predetermined theology in mind, and therefore interprets the text from that pre-disposition. When he teaches the art of biblical interpretation, called hermeneutics, at his seminary, he tells his students NOT to interpret the text that way! He says to let the text speak for itself and interpret it clearly and accurately as to what the writer is saying. In other words, what does the text say? What is the writer attempting to convey to his audience? How are the words in Greek normally translated and interpreted? But that is not what John does whenever it comes to the Gifts of the Spirit, or even healing in the book of James.

Listen to Gordon Fee's comments in the margin of his notes in his work "God's Empowering Presence"on the miracles which were taking place in the Galatian churches, and Dr. MacArthur's view: *"As MacArthur who suggests that "miracles" here really means "powers" of basically non-miraculous kinds, or that otherwise it refers to past miracles, at the beginning of their life in Christ. Such comments have very little to do with Paul and very much to do with theological pre-judgments."*

I am not sure that John has ever experienced a church service where he himself has let God use him to give a Word of Wisdom, a Word of Knowledge, or a Prophecy of encouragement, comfort, or strengthening. Oh, he has done it all his life through the teaching of God's word; no one would deny that. In fact, I think he is one of the best at preaching and teaching. But the Gift of Prophecy is more than simply explaining a text. It is an inspiration from the Holy Spirit concerning an individual, a situation, or something needing to be said to the whole church which God gives at that moment to be spoken through one who has this Gift. I will give you biblical explanations and biblical examples of the proper definitions of the Gifts of the Spirit in later chapters.

Gordon Fee goes on to say, *"The evidence from 1 and 2 Thessalonians and elsewhere, indicates that prophecy was a regular and expected phenomenon in his (Paul's) churches; 1 Corinthians indicates that speaking in tongues was also a part of the broad experience of Spirit phenomena. This text shows that what Paul elsewhere calls "signs and wonders" was also a regular and expected expression of their life in the Spirit. What we cannot know from this distance, of course, is all Paul would have understood by the phrase "works miracles among you." But similar phrasing elsewhere in the corpus suggests a variety of supernatural phenomena, including healings."*

Because the basis of John's theology of the Gifts is faulty to begin with, John is also unable to define them properly. That is why John states in the introduction of his book Strange Fire, "The 'Holy Spirit' found in the vast majority of charismatic teaching and practice bears no resemblance to the true Spirit of God as revealed in scripture." This may be true in some of the larger independent ministries and other churches where things are done out of order, but it is not true of Christians in churches where there is balance and a genuine operation of the Gifts.

I have been in quite a few churches where the gifts operate as God desires them to, and people are truly blessed, strengthened, encouraged, and corrected. In fact, that is exactly how they operate in the church I pastor. No one, including myself, wants anything that is phony, made up, contrived, or that is not the real presence and power of God. None of us want that. But there is a real power from God through the Holy Spirit which is not allowed or even believed in many church services today. Let's begin by properly defining what these nine Gifts are and how the Bible itself explains how they function.

CHAPTER 5

DEFINING THE NINE GIFTS OF 1 CORINTHIANS 12

Let's talk about two different problems concerning 1) how the Gifts of the Spirit function, and 2) properly defining what the gifts are.

First, as we have been talking about in Chapter 1, Cessationists believe most, if not all, the Gifts of the Spirit are no longer in operation from the death of the last Apostle until now. They randomly pick and choose which ones have ceased to exist and which ones continue today, with absolutely zero scriptural support.

For example, John MacArthur states that tongues, interpretation of tongues, miracles and healings have all ceased (thus the term Cessationists) to operate in the body of Christ today. How he comes up with this "list" is still beyond me. He cannot properly quote even one scripture to support this.

Secondly, he sets about to re-define the other five remaining Gifts listed in 1 Corinthians 9 and completely misses how the Bible itself defines them, and he then makes it sound as though they are mere human abilities and not Gifts which the Holy Spirit gives.

Let's look at these nine Gifts and let the Bible itself define what they are and how they operate.

Please note that in this chapter I am not yet arguing for the continuation of the Gifts, that will come in a later chapter. Right now I want to make sure you understand what the Gifts are and how they operate.

PROPHECY IN THE NEW TESTAMENT

Let's begin with prophecy. This Gift has been more misunderstood, redefined, and misused than any other Gift, except maybe the Gift of Tongues. I will make this as simple as possible for it is the one Gift of which Paul said, "Follow the way of love, and eagerly desire the Gifts of the Spirit; especially the Gift of **PROPHECY** (1 Corinthians 14:1)! There must have been a reason the Holy Spirit wanted this Gift to be prolific in the church and wanted all believers to have it..

Prophecy is **not** the same as preaching or teaching. Romans 12:6-7 makes that abundantly clear. "We have different gifts, according to the grace given us. If a man's gift is prophesying, let him use it in proportion to his faith"... "If anyone teaches, let him teach." One Gift is expounding what the Word says (teaching), the other is speaking what the Spirit is saying (prophecy). One is giving an explanation of what has been written, the other is sharing a sense of what the Spirit is saying. That isn't contradiction, it is clarification!

Now, I am only using these two gifts, teaching and prophesying as examples. None of us as true evangelical Charismatics would ever deny that what is written in the Bible is God's infallible Word. Most of us (I say most, because I do not know what every Charismatic preacher believes or teaches) believe that what is written in the Bible is the absolute authority for life and doctrine. God's Word is forever settled in heaven (Ps 119:89). But what the 'Spirit speaks' is a little harder to discern. Anyone can say, "The Spirit told me..." But how do we gauge that statement as to its accuracy? The same way the early church did, by examining what is being said. I agree and admit that there are so-called Christian leaders out there who are saying things which are not from the Spirit of God and do not line up with the clear teachings of scripture. These men and women must be rebuked and corrected. But that is NOT EVERY CHARISMATIC PREACHER..

I believe Wayne Grudem in his work entitled "Systematic Theology," subtitled 'an introduction to Biblical doctrine,' is very similar to my definition of this gift, when he says, *"Although several definitions have been given for the gift of prophecy, a fresh examination of the New Testament teaching on this gift will show that it should not defined as predicting the future...but rather as 'telling something that God has spontaneously brought to mind.'"* I would add that, at times, it can be predictive of something in the future if God so chooses. I will develop this further below.

So let's look at the Gift of Prophecy by beginning with the father of John the Baptist. His name was Zechariah.

The angel Gabriel appeared to him and told him his wife, Elizabeth, who was barren, was going to have a child. That was hard for Zechariah to receive since she was a very old woman. In fact, Zechariah doubted what Gabriel had said and because he doubted, Gabriel told him he would not be able to speak for a while. That's exactly what happened; he couldn't say a word until after John was born.

Then Zechariah, Luke records, prophesied. If you read his "prophecy" closely, you will see that the first two-thirds of it are him simply quoting scripture. Then he shares some future events, and then he speaks some words of encouragement. My point is, people only think of prophecy as predicting future events, but it is often much simpler and much more encouraging than that. Paul says in 1 Corinthians 14:3, prophecy is for encouragement, comfort, and edification (building people up).

Most of the time when people have "prophesied" in our church, they are either quoting a verse and giving an interpretation or sense of the meaning of that verse, or speaking words of encouragement, correction, direction, warning, or a reminder of God's love. Prophecy can really be that simple. It would have to be, since Paul wanted everyone to do it. However, I have also witnessed people giving a Prophecy that actually set things in motion in someone's life. By that I mean, something had died in them, or had been hindered from coming to pass, or maybe they made a mistake or fell into sin, and it "paused" what God wanted to do in them. When someone under the anointing speaks prophetically to them, the blessings in their life are now set in motion again, and they were able to pick up where they left off before they were stalled.

The scriptures are replete with these kinds of examples. Isaiah 40:1-2 is just one example. Isaiah says, "'Comfort, comfort My people,' says your God. Speak kindly to the heart of Jerusalem and proclaim to her that her warfare has ended, that her iniquity has been removed."

Isaiah was speaking the end of something that had been blocking Israel's blessings because of sins and God was now ready to reinstitute the blessings to her once again. When the Spirit of God inspires an anointed vessel of His to speak to His people, things are set in motion in the Spirit and also in the soul of the person it is spoken to.

Whenever someone speaks words of prophecy, we the church are to "weigh carefully" what is said and judge whether or not it lines up with God's word. If it doesn't, we say, "I don't believe that is what the Spirit of God is saying." We don't take him outside in the parking lot and stone him! However, when someone begins to state things of a predictive nature and they don't come to pass, I start reaching for a rock myself!

I believe what bothers the Cessationists' camp is when Charismatics or anyone else for that matter, prophesy about future events and time-tables and these things don't come to pass. Whenever this happens Cessationists have wrongly concluded that ALL prophecy is no longer for today. (The Jehovah Witness group "prophesied" that Jesus was coming back in 1914 and again in 1925, neither of which obviously came to pass).

This is very unfortunate. I listen carefully when anyone says thus and so is going to happen. I know time will prove them right or wrong. Unfortunately, far too often, they have been wrong. That is what makes that person, and unfortunately the gift also, suspect. I understand why the Cessationists feel this way. But that doesn't mean the gift of prophecy isn't alive and well, it means that individual is dead wrong!

Yes, danger comes when someone tries to give a predictive word about something or someone that can only be judged by whether or not it comes to pass. These are the types of prophecies which concern me. These are the ones for which, in the Old Testament, prophets would get stoned to death when they were wrong. I also have a deep sensitivity to people who try to give what I call "**personal prophecies.**"

This is when someone tells an individual that such and such is going to happen to them or for them. I have seen these types of words do damage to people's lives. They believe that this so-called prophecy is spoken by God to them through this person, and they take it to be as authoritative as the Word of God itself. And it is not!

Only time can tell if what they said is true. This is where I teach our people to be very careful about ever saying "**THUS SAITH THE LORD.**" If ever someone does use this terminology of "God said," they'd better have a nearly spotless record of being right; otherwise their integrity and accuracy are brought into question, and rightly so. But let me clarify. I said near spotless because again, Paul said to

77

let two or three prophets speak and let the others weigh carefully what has been said. That means, there was NOT 100% accuracy in all the prophecies. Again, Paul said to the Thessalonians, "Do not despise prophesying. Test all things and hold on to the good..." Translation, "Listen carefully and only accept that which is accurate."

However, because these unfortunate "so-called prophecies" have been many, Cessationists have concluded that prophecy no longer functions in the church and therefore they have created a theology which makes it impossible for this gift to exist by emphatically teaching people it doesn't. Other Cessationists simply redefine what the gift actually is, which I will address below.

John MacArthur states in his book that Charismatics "claim" to be able to prophesy, by which he means, they receive a message or inspiration from the Holy Spirit, and when asked if that message is from God and equal in authority to scripture, Charismatics would say "no." Of course no evangelical Christian in his right mind would say "yes." But then John deduces that if the word of prophecy supposedly is from the Holy Spirit, which would make it AUTHORITATIVE like the Word of God, then it must be EQUAL to the Word of God. Of course we answer, "no, it isn't."

The point John is trying to make (a poor one I might add) is that if prophecy today were from the Holy

Spirit, it would be as authoritative as the Word of God itself. As I said above, what the Spirit of God speaks outside of the Word is more subjective, and therefore it must be weighed and judged. Then Dr. MacArthur says that if the prophecy is from God and yet not as authoritative as the Word of God, it really can't be of God. Poor deduction, Sir.

Again, Wayne Grudem says, "Yet there certainly were prophets prophesying in many local congregations after the death of the apostles. It seems that they did not have authority equal to the apostles, and the authors of scripture knew that. The conclusion is that prophecies today are not 'the words of God' either," meaning, equal to God's known word, the Holy Scriptures.

Let me explain:

Right before John had his Strange Fire conference in 2013, after having spoken to him on numerous occasions before that, including flying down to speak with him in person at Valencia Country Club, I also had this conversation with him on the phone. I had listened to his CD which was done with Mr. Phil Johnson, a good Christian brother and dear friend and colleague of John's, about Charismatics (The CD is #GTY 137, dated 2012). John made the same argument on the CD that I just stated in the paragraph above, namely, if someone prophesies, is it equal in authority to the Word of God? I explained clearly to John that not even the Bible says PROPHECY is of the same authority as the Word of God.

I said to John, "Philip had four daughters who prophesied (Acts 21:9). Do we have any of those prophecies written down in scripture?" He said "No." I said, "Do we have any of the prophecies which were obviously spoken in the church at Corinth (1 Corinth 14) or the ones implied were spoken in the church at Thessalonica (1 Thess 5:19-22) written down?" He said "No" again. I said to him that if the prophecies which were spoken by those people and in those churches were real (and we both agreed they were) and we have none of them written down as "The Word of God" then New Testament prophecy can't be equal with scripture, but it can still be from the Holy Spirit. He said, **"Point taken."**

I then asked John to allow me to sit on the panel at his "Strange Fire" conference as one who would represent the other side, namely the "Charismatics," to which he quickly said, "No, I'm not going to do that." The reason that he and Phil Johnson are able to get away with these kinds of statements is because there is no one in the room who can argue their points. They are just sitting in the studio or wherever they are recording these CDs and talking as two men who agree with each other.

But if someone were there who could say, "Hey wait a minute, that's not accurate" it would be a different story. Didn't Paul say to the Corinthians, "We do not dare to classify or compare ourselves with some who commend themselves. When they measure themselves by themselves and compare themselves with themselves, they are not wise" (2Cor 12:12).

But is that any different than listening to the teaching or preaching of the Word of God and judging what is being said? Isn't that how we determine errant teaching from accurate teaching? By listening and judging? Hasn't Dr. MacArthur done just that in his work "Strange Fire?" He listened to or read things that have been spoken by Charismatic leaders and then he judged them as to their accuracy. Perfectly acceptable. On many of his judgments I agree with him.

But is it so far-fetched to think that the Holy Spirit can speak something specific to someone and through someone which actually is from Him, the Holy Spirit? It happened all through the early church as recorded in scripture. It only CAN'T happen if we say it can't. But is that what scripture really says?

So the real issues with what John MacArthur is speaking and writing about as I see it are threefold:

1) He mentions some people whom he qualifies as Charismatic who have said or are saying things which

are incorrect and heretical, but uses all-inclusive language to include all Charismatics.

2) John absolutely does not believe in the gifts of the Spirit being in operation today, including speaking in other tongues.

3) John's explanation of the gifts of the Spirit is inaccurate and shows his lack of having ever operated in the genuine gifts, which leads him to a faulty definition of them.

Here is something to consider; If the prophets spoke NEW REVELATION every time they spoke, and this revelation was supposed to be authoritative like scripture, can anyone produce those documents? In other words, we have no writings from the New Testament prophets. None. At least none that John MacArthur or anyone else would call scripture. We all agree that the canon of scripture is closed. There are no new books to be added, including the Book of Mormon or the Quran. But we have nothing written of which the New Testament prophets spoke.

For example, in Acts 15, Silas and Judas are both called prophets. Yet we have nothing in writing that they ever said or "prophesied." So then, not everything spoken by the Holy Spirit through His vessels is equal to scripture. Yet, Ephesians 2:19-20 says that the foundation of the church was built on the authority of what the apostles and prophets said. My point where John said "point taken" is that we can still prophesy today without it being man-inspired on one hand, or as authoritative as scripture on the other. So what is the proof test? Judge and test all things (1Thess 5:19).

When we are referring to New Testament prophecy, there are two different meanings or kinds of prophecies. One kind of prophecy can be fore-telling. For example, Agabus, in Acts 21, took Paul's belt and said, "The Holy Spirit says, 'In this way the Jews of Jerusalem will bind the owner of this belt and will hand him over to the gentiles.'" If that happened today in our churches, the only way to "test" it is to see if it comes to pass. Here is the problem: If an individual stands up and says "Thus saith the Lord" concerning something which is to take place in the future, and he ends up being wrong, it undermines the people's confidence the next time he says thus saith the Lord. Not to mention, in the Old Testament he could or would have been stoned. However, let me give you some things to think about.

In the Old Testament they had what was called "The company of the prophets" (See 2 Kings Chapter 2 and chapter 6). It seems these were schools (seminaries?) where the prophets stayed and were taught to hear and understand the voice of the Lord. In chapter 2 it says the company of the prophets knew that Elijah was going to be taken up by the Lord. In chapter 5, the place where they stayed and were trained, presumably by Elisha, was too small and they wanted to build a bigger place to live.

My point here is this: They learned and grew in their Gift of Prophecy by practice and training from a teacher, namely Elisha. Now I know there is some conjecture on my part due to the limited knowledge of the company of the prophets, but it makes perfect sense that they had to learn the distinction between the voice of the Lord and "what was bad pizza from the night before!" Do you think that in their development they at first may have missed the voice of God? I think it is possible. And by the way, we have none of their writings of things they prophesied!

So let's carry that thought into the New Testament era. When Paul says that two or three prophets should speak and the others should weigh carefully what is said, he is saying that as a person is developing in this gift they may not always be accurate. As much as that may bother John MacArthur and other non-Charismatics, you can't deny that is what Paul said. Now please understand, I am NOT saying that it is OK for someone to "prophesy" and get it wrong. Not even close.

I teach our people to be very careful about ever saying "thus saith the Lord." I have been saved for 34 years and I have rarely said those words because I do understand the seriousness of their implications. But at the same time, when it has been a fore-telling of something that I was sure God was saying through me to another individual, I spoke it as a "thus saith the Lord," knowing full well I had better be right.

Personal examples

For example, we have a lady in our church whom the Lord is using to begin a ministry of rescuing young girls and boys out of the sex slave trade in our area. When she came to me to ask me whether she should go forward in doing this (she is a high level employee for Cisco systems), I told her that she could do this. I told her that God was going to use her in greater ways than she could ever imagine.

I also told her that God was going to take her ministry nation-wide and open up many doors with high-level people in government and the corporate sector as well, and she would be shown much favor and people would give financially to help underwrite her efforts. Since that day almost three years ago, all those things have come to pass. I knew that when I said those things to her she trusted me as her pastor and that I was not one who goes around always saying "thus saith the Lord."

Another young lady in our church who is finishing Bible college at the time of writing this book, reminded me that I had prophesied to her when she was much younger, that she would be an instructor of young women in many different parts of the world. That is already taking place in her life. Because I was speaking of future events which were to come to pass in her life, we had to wait a few years to see if they would come to pass, and guess what, they have. Again, I don't say these kinds of things all the time, but there have been quite a few more incidents I could share with you.

Two Gifts at a time

To be sure, at times, more than one gift can be in operation at the same time. I have been given a word of knowledge from the Holy Spirit concerning someone and then immediately gave them what I would call a prophecy.

Case in point: A young lady was in my prayer line when I was ministering in another church and as I began to pray for her, the Lord showed me a picture of her concerning music (Word of Knowledge). I asked her if she was involved in music and instantly she began to cry. She said her mom traveled around ministering in song and she used to go and minister with her, but had stopped because she was somewhat backslidden. I then told her that God loved her and He was calling her back and wanted her to begin again ministering in music with her mom, and that God was going to use her mightily again (Prophecy). She left that night having rededicated her life to the Lord and said she was going to let God use her as He had done before. Her countenance was completely changed. Two Gifts were working together; The Word of Knowledge and Prophecy. This has happened literally hundreds of times in my ministry. How could I know those things? It wasn't spooky, or only for the "high and mighty." Rather, it was simply being open to what the Spirit of God wanted to say to His daughter (her) through His son (me). But if you believe it can't happen today, it won't.

But let's continue defining Prophecy.

In Acts 11:28 you again find Agabus with a group of prophets coming down from Jerusalem to Antioch in Acts 11:28. He speaks a word of Prophecy (foretelling) about a severe famine that would spread over the entire Roman world. The only way to test that Prophecy was to wait and see if it would take place. Guess what, we know it did because Luke says "This happened during the reign of Claudius."

This foretelling kind of Prophecy is tough to judge because only time will tell if what they said is true or not. When an individual says something which is supposedly from the Holy Spirit and they end up being wrong, this casts a shadow of doubt as to both their validity and the validity of the gift itself the next time they speak. But when someone is starting out in this gift older, more mature saints should help them discern the voice of the Holy Spirit and guide them in how it is to operate.

The other definition of Prophecy in the New Testament seems to be much less demonstrative but equally important and much more prevalent than the fore-telling kind of Prophecy. Some have labeled it "simple prophecy." This kind of Prophecy is for the strengthening, comfort and encouragement of the individual or the congregation (1 Cor 14:3).

Please keep in mind what Paul said in 1 Cor 14:1, "Eagerly desire spiritual gifts, ESPECIALLY the gift of prophecy." And again in 1 Thess 5:19-21, "Do not put out the Spirit's fire; do not treat prophecies with contempt. Test everything. Hold on to the good."

One cannot deny that Prophecy was a Gift given by the Holy Spirit and that we the church have the ability to allow it or hinder it in our public gathering times. And whenever it was in operation through anyone in the church, or through all, it was to be judged and weighed carefully as to what was spoken so that if someone had "missed it," the church wouldn't be led into error.

It wasn't or isn't something to be done only by the apostles or prophets but rather given to and used by all as the Holy Spirit desires. In fact, you and I are to eagerly desire this gift above all the other gifts. Some non-Charismatics have not only quenched the Holy Spirit in this way, but they have put out the Holy Spirit's fire altogether.

So, what are we learning? The Holy Spirit **DOES** give Gifts to the church. Each person is to show self control and use their Gift at the proper time and in the proper way. And this includes everyone, from the Prophet in the church to the average lay person. Everyone is to listen and then judge whether this was something from God, or just something from the flesh.

Listen as Paul continues talking about the prophets. In 1 Cor 14: 29-33 he says; "Two or three prophets should speak, and the others should weigh carefully what is said. And if a revelation comes to someone who is sitting down, the first speaker should stop. For you can all prophesy in turn so that everyone may be instructed and encouraged. The spirits of the prophets are subject to the control of the prophets. For God is not a God of disorder but of peace." Or how about verse 39, "Therefore my brothers, be EAGER to prophesy, and do NOT forbid speaking in tongues. But everything should be done in a fitting and orderly way."

Or again, Paul said, "I thank God that I speak in tongues more than all of you" (vs.18). Like it or not, Paul was a Charismatic of the first order! Or how about this, "Now to each one the manifestation of the Spirit is given for the common good" (1 Corinthians 12:7). These were not given to just the apostles, at least not in this letter to the Corinthians. No scholar worth his salt would say this was written only to apostles. It was spoken to the church body as a whole.

This was written to the average Christian sitting in the church. In other words, to whomever the Holy Spirit wanted to give these Gifts. And each manifestation (Gift) of the Spirit was given so that everyone could profit from them. Did I mention these gifts were given to a very carnal, immature, and divisive group of Christians? WHY WOULD GOD give His precious

Gifts to such a rag-tag bunch of people? Why would he let them be the ones to authenticate His beautiful and gracious Gifts? I guess one could ask why God would even allow His Spirit to live in people like that? Didn't Paul say to them, "THEREFORE, YOU DO NOT LACK ANY SPIRITUAL GIFT…"(1Cor 1:7). I will let you muse over that for a minute.

In fact, think about this: Samson was one of the most anointed men in the Old Testament. He did amazing miracles and showed feats of strength that few if any have ever followed. He killed 1,000 men with a donkey's jawbone. Caught 300 foxes and tied their tails together and started fields on fire. He broke ropes like rubber bands and tore a lion with his hands like one would tear a young goat (Judges 14). The Bible says the Spirit of the Lord came on him with great power (Judges 14:6).

Yet, this man was steeped in sexual sin! The first thing the Bible says about him is that he saw there a young Philistine woman (14:1). This man had a weakness for women and a serious sexual addiction. Why would God validate His power and precious Gifts through such a wayward man? Because the Gifts which the Holy Spirit gives serve a different function than the fruit of the Spirit.

God didn't want Samson to be a sinful man. God had his parents raise him as a Nazarite all the days of his life. God wanted him to live a holy and separated life away from sin. But God had already determined to give him his powerful Gifts of miracles with undeniable feats of strength.

Unfortunately, Samson did not equate the grace-gifts God gave him with living a holy life. He thought he could live any way he wanted with no ramifications for his actions. God was merciful and patient with him for a good while, but God will not be mocked (Galatians 6:7).

Prophecy doesn't have to be some deep spiritual revelation of what is going to happen to the nations, or who the next president will be (although if the Holy Spirit wanted to reveal those things, He certainly could). It is speaking words of encouragement, comfort, or edification to an individual or the entire church. It can be quoting and giving a sense of a scripture, or reminding people how much God loves them.

So I say to you what the Holy Spirit said through Paul to the church in Corinth; "Eagerly desire the Gifts of the Spirit, and especially the Gift of prophecy" (1 Corinthians 14:1).

CHAPTER 6

THE WORD OF KNOWLEDGE AND THE WORD OF WISDOM

Remember, these are pneumatikos, or "spiritual things" in the simplest English translation. In the Greek language the wording here can be in a masculine or neuter sense. I know, "What does that mean?" If it is in the masculine sense it means a person; things of the (Holy) Spirit. If it is in the neuter sense it is a thing; concerning spiritual things. Context determines the best meaning. In this case here in 1 Corinthians 12, it is in the neuter, meaning "concerning spiritual things"…

So, these nine gifts are spiritual things, or things which the Spirit gives. The word "gifts" is not in the original Greek letter to the Corinthians in verse 1, it was added by the translators due to the fact that the word "gifts" is found later in verse 4. By the way, the word "gifts" in Greek in the 4th verse is the word 'char-is-ma,' meaning "grace gift."

Paul starts with the "Word of Knowledge." This is a Gift which the Holy Spirit gives to whom He wants and when He wants, to an individual or individuals. It is something the Spirit of God reveals that otherwise you couldn't or wouldn't know. In other words, no one told you, you didn't read about it or hear about it, the Spirit of God just showed you for a distinct purpose and reason.

Let's look at some Biblical examples of the Word of Knowledge in operation.

We could start all the way back in the Garden of Eden when Adam and Eve learned from God about eating from the tree of the knowledge of good and evil. They knew if they ate of it they would surely die. How did they know that? They didn't read about it in the newspaper, or learn it at the local college, or by even reading a medical journal on fatal diseases. No. God directly told them Himself.

When Noah built the Ark, how did he know to build it and that it was going to rain, and that the world would be flooded? He wasn't a meteorologist, he didn't check the weather report on the local news channel or even have access to the "Farmers Almanac." God told him exactly what was coming and what to do about it. All the other people on the planet knew nothing about this. In fact, up until that time, it had never even rained!

We could talk about things God revealed to Abraham, Isaac, and even to Jacob, about what God had told them. And how about Rebecca? How did she know that she was going to have twins and that the older would serve the younger? God told her something that she could not have known ahead of time unless the Spirit of God showed it to her. They did not have ultrasound machines at that time.

We could go on and on about Joseph knowing things like seven years of plenty and then seven years of famine. We could talk about Joseph knowing he was going to die before the promises God had made to his dad and forefathers concerning leaving Egypt and going to the Promised Land before they ever came to fulfillment, and how he made the Israelites promise to take his bones with them so he would not remain buried in Egypt. How would he know that?

You might be thinking right now, "But these all happened BEFORE the completion of the New Testament." Yes, but wait, we are talking about what the Word of Knowledge is, not whether or not this particular Gift still operates today. I promise I will get to that next. I'm trying to let the Bible define for us what this Gift is. Remember I said, it is the ability the Holy Spirit gives to someone to know something they couldn't otherwise have known.

I'm not even going to mention ALL the Words of Knowledge that Moses received. You know, to go and set God's people free, that Pharaoh would harden his heart, that God would do great miracles to demonstrate His power... It goes on and on.

ELIJAH

For the sake of time, let's look at the ministries of Elijah and Elisha. The story of Elijah begins in 1 Kings 17 and goes through 2 Kings Chapter 2. It begins with Elijah getting a "Word of Knowledge" from God concerning it not raining on the land for over three years. How did he know that? Was he a meteorologist? OK. OK. I know, you get it already.

Then he goes to a brook where birds are commanded by God to feed him and he would drink from the brook. How would he know that? Then after a while the brook dried up and he went to a town where he knew a dying widow would feed him. How would he know that? I mean, "God, if you are going to provide food for me don't let it be by a bird and a widow. A nice millionaire family at the Country Club would be just fine, thank you." How could he know a starving widow would feed him?

Another time, the wicked King Ahab decided he wanted a man's vineyard so he could use it for a garden because it was close to his palace. The man who owned it, Naboth, didn't want to give it up because it had belonged to his family for generations. Ahab started pouting and went home and told his wife, the even more wicked, Queen Jezebel. She told him she would get it for him. So she came up with a deceptive plan and had Naboth killed and Ahab then took over the man's property.

The Lord then told Elijah what had happened (a Word of Knowledge) and to meet Ahab and say to him "Have you not murdered a man and seized his property?" 1 Kings 21:17-19. How did Elijah know that?

ELISHA

Let's look at the ministry of Elisha. By the way, I will show you that the Gifts which the Holy Spirit gives cannot be used any time you want. God reveals things as He wills. Is that clear? If it's not clear, I will show you.

Elisha comes on the scene in the Bible in 1 Kings 19:16, near the end of Elijah's story. You remember what happened. Elijah is taken up to heaven in a whirlwind and chariots and horses of fire. Well, his successor is the Prophet Elisha. Do you remember what Elisha asks of Elijah? He says "I want a double portion of the Spirit which is on you." Elijah says to him, "If you see me when I am taken up, it shall be yours" (2 Kings 2:9-10).

By the way, how did Elijah know that he was going to be taken up? Did he get a phone call from NASA? Did the president send him on a special covert mission? Did aliens come down and tell him and then transport him to another planet? No. God told him something he could not have known UNLESS the Spirit of God had revealed it to him. But back to Elisha.

God directed the steps of Elisha just like he did Elijah's.

In 2 Kings 4:8-36, there was an elderly couple who were people of financial means, and God touched their hearts to provide a room with a lamp, a table, a chair, and a bed in it, so any time Elisha was passing through their town he would have a place to stay. (There is a whole sermon in this story, but I will save that for another day or another book).

Because of this couple's kindness to Elisha, he wanted to do something special for them. To make a nice story short, he told the woman that she would get pregnant and have a child within a year. How would he know that? Now I know he was a prophet and that's what prophets do; they prophesy things to come. By the way, I will also show you from scripture that often times the Gifts work in tandem with other Gifts of the Spirit.

So, the lady has a son, and the boy begins to grow. When he gets to a certain age, one day his head starts to hurt him real bad. He cries out to his dad who of course calls out for the mom, and later that day the child dies, probably from a brain aneurysm. She quickly goes to find Elisha who is now in big trouble because this mother is very upset with Elisha for telling her that she would have a son in the first place. And now for the child to die was simply too painful for her.

She approaches Elisha to tell him what has happened. Elisha has a servant named Gehazi who travels with him. Gehazi goes to push the woman away from Elisha, but Elisha says to leave her alone for "THE LORD HAS NOT TOLD ME WHAT HAS HAPPENED TO HER." Did you get that? The Lord had not made it known to him. In other words, the Word of Knowledge does not operate whenever you want it to. It operates when the LORD says it will operate. Period!

One more story concerning Elisha is found in 2 Kings Chapter 5. A Gentile man by the name of Naaman who was a valuable leader for the king, had leprosy. He had a Jewish servant girl whom he had captured and she told him "If only my master would see the prophet (Elisha) who is in Samaria! He would cure him of his leprosy." (That was NOT a word of knowledge. She knew Elisha was in Samaria and she knew God used him to do miracles. She was simply giving Naaman information which was common knowledge.)

So Naaman left for Samaria with gifts of money and clothes and arrived where Elisha was. After going to see the king of Israel first, he went to Elisha who told him to dip himself in the Jordan river seven times and he would be healed. Naaman finally consented and when he dipped the seventh time, he was instantly healed of his leprosy. In his gratitude, he wanted to give Elisha money but Elisha said "No thank you." Gehazi, Elisha's servant, heard the whole exchange between the two of them and thought to himself, "My master was too easy on him by not accepting from him what he brought." So Gehazi secretly went after Naaman and lied to him, saying that Elisha sent him back because two prophets unexpectedly showed up and they could use his gifts. Naaman obliged him and Gehazi hid the gifts from Elisha.

However, through a Word of Knowledge, Elisha knew exactly what had transpired between Gehazi and Naaman, so when Gehazi returned Elisha said, "Did not my spirit go with you when the man got down from his chariot to meet you?" In other words, Elisha knew something (Word of Knowledge) that he could only know if the Spirit of God had shown him. This is the Bible's definition of a Word of Knowledge.

Let's look at some more examples of this Gift in operation in the New Testament. Remember, right now I'm not arguing for whether or not these Gifts still operate in the church, I am simply giving you the proper definition of what these Gifts are by showing you some Biblical accounts of them in operation.

JESUS OPERATING IN THE WORD OF KNOWLEDGE

Jesus operated in the Word of Knowledge on a regular basis. You might say, "But Jesus is God. Maybe He did do those things, but it doesn't mean we can." Again, in this chapter, I'm not arguing for the Gifts being in operation, I'm simply defining what the Gifts are by giving you Biblical examples of how they function. Keep this in mind for now. I will argue for the continuation of the Gifts in another chapter.

When Jesus was about to triumphantly enter the city, he told two of his disciples to go to the village ahead of them and they would find a donkey tied with her colt next to her. He told them if anyone asked them why they were taking (stealing?) them (which is exactly what happened) they were to say that the Lord needed them. Mark 11:1-6

How did Jesus know these things? Well, I guess he could have arranged them in advance, but we all know that isn't the case. Jesus was operating in the Word of Knowledge. Knowing something by the Holy Spirit that He couldn't otherwise have known.

In another story found in Mark 14:12-16, Jesus wanted to have the last supper with his disciples before he died. He told them to go into the city and they would see a man carrying a water jar. Follow him to a house and he will show you a large upper room where we will eat the Passover. The reason this man would stand out in the city is because women usually carried the water jars. Guess what? That is exactly what happened.

How did Jesus know these events would happen? Had he pre-arranged them? Did someone set them up for him in advance? Or, did the Spirit of God speak to him something which no human being could have known, called a Word of Knowledge? I think you are starting to get it now. I could share many more examples of what this Gift is in the life of Jesus, but let's move ahead to the book of Acts.

PETER OPERATING IN THE WORD OF KNOWLEDGE IN THE BOOK OF ACTS

Please remember that a Word of Knowledge can come by an inspiration of the holy Spirit through an inner witness, a dream, vision, or a trance.

Peter, in Acts chapter 5 had a Word of Knowledge (or two) concerning Ananias and his wife Sapphira. They had sold a piece of property and brought the money to the disciples for them to distribute to the poor in the church, a common practice in the early church (see Acts 2:45, 4:36-37). Yet, Peter knew they were lying and that they had held back some of the money for themselves. They were perfectly free to give as much or as little as they wanted from the sale, or even none, if they so desired.

But they wanted to keep some of the money for their own use so they lied to Peter about the true amount. The Holy Spirit made Peter aware of this by the Word of Knowledge and Peter confronted them and spoke their demise into existence. Both Ananias and his wife Sapphira died for lying to the Holy Spirit by lying to Peter. Again, Peter knew something which he didn't learn by human sources.

ANANIAS GETS A WORD OF KNOWLEDGE IN THE BOOK OF ACTS

When Paul was saved in Acts chapter 9, another man named Ananias (not the one killed in Acts chapter 5), received a word from the Lord that there was a man named Saul (Paul) who was staying at the house of a man named Judas who lived on Straight Street (Acts 9:11). The Lord gave Ananias instructions about what to do and say to Paul.

How would Ananias know these things? How would Ananias know Paul was at this man's house on Straight Street? How would he know that Paul was in prayer and was seeing him, Ananias, coming to where he was? This is the Word of Knowledge in action. Again, the scriptures are replete with these stories and examples of HOW this Gift of the Spirit works. It is the ability to know something you did not learn through human or natural means. It is a Gift from the Holy Spirit. In fact, in this case with Ananias, both the Word of Knowledge and the Word of Wisdom are working in tandem. He was told something he couldn't have known (Word of Knowledge) and was given instructions from the Lord on what to do (Word of Wisdom)..

The Word of Knowledge and the Word of Wisdom work the same way as Prophecy, Tongues, Miracles and all the Gifts mentioned in 1 Corinthians 12. They are supernatural endowments of the Holy Spirit distributed to whom He wills and when He wills.

WORD OF WISDOM

The Gift of the Word of Wisdom is not simple human wisdom which means someone is smarter than the other believers in his group. As Christians, we all have access to wisdom because we see things through the lens of scripture.

But this is not the Word of Wisdom which Paul is talking about in 1 Corinthians 12.

For example, in Ephesians 1:15-19, Paul said that he was praying for them that "God would give them the spirit of wisdom, that the eyes of their understanding would be opened…"

Again, in Colossians 2:3, Paul said, "All the treasures of wisdom and knowledge are in Christ Jesus…"

In the book of James 1:5, he said, "If any man lacks wisdom, let him ask of God who gives it freely to all who ask…"

This is what I call increased wisdom to understand the Word, understand all about Jesus, and to operate more effectively in everyday life. But the Gift from the Holy Spirit called a Word of Wisdom is something which the Spirit reveals in a given moment or situation to whomever He wants when He wants.

Examples of the Word of Wisdom are when the Lord, the Spirit, tells people what they should do or how they should do something. For example, in 2 Samuel 5, the Philistines came up to attack David. He asked the Lord if he should engage them in battle. The Lord said "Go," I will surely hand them over to you." This was a Word of Knowledge. But the Philistines came to attack them again a couple of verses later and David asked the Lord again. This time the Lord gave David a Word of Wisdom, or told him what he should do. The Lord said, "Do not go straight up, but circle around behind them and attack them in front of the Balsam trees. As soon as you hear the sound of marching in the tops of the Balsam trees, move quickly, because that will mean the Lord has gone out in front of you to strike the Philistine army" (vss. 22-25). **A Word of Knowledge gives information and A Word of Wisdom gives direction.**

These are completely **DIFFERENT** definitions of the gifts of the Spirit than those given by the Cessationists camps. Listen to John MacArthur's definition from his commentary on 1 Corinthians 12: *A thorough examination will yield the truth that spiritual gifts fill two major purposes: the permanent gifts edify the church and the temporary gifts are signs to confirm the Word of God. God will continue to give the permanent gifts to believers for the duration of the church age, and those gifts are to be ministered by His people at all times in the life of the church. Those gifts include first the speaking or verbal gifts - prophecy, knowledge, wisdom, teaching, and exhortation, and, second, the serving or nonverbal gifts-leadership, helps, giving, mercy, faith, and discernment. The temporary sign gifts were limited to the apostolic age and therefore ceased after that time. Those gifts included miracles, healing, languages, and the interpretation of languages. The purpose of temporary sign gifts was to authenticate the apostolic message as the Word of God, until the time when the scriptures,*

107

His written Word, were completed and became self-authenticating.

Let's look at what John says

First, he makes a distinction between what he calls permanent gifts and temporary gifts. Where does he get this list from? He says miracles, healings, languages, and the interpretation of languages ceased after the apostles. What scriptures does he base this on? None! He also says they were only in use until the New Testament was completed. Really? Not even the New Testament knows about this.

I do like that at least he says prophecy, word of knowledge, and word of wisdom are still in operation today, but then he improperly defines what those gifts are and how they operate. Look at what he says about the Word of Wisdom: "In the apostolic age it may have been revelation at times." I believe what he means by "revelation at times" is what I will show below in how this Gift actually works.

But then Dr. MacArthur goes on and completely misses the description of what this gift is and how it works. He continues, *"Wisdom, then, refers basically to applying truths discovered, to the ability to make skillful and practical application of the truth to life situations. Communicating wisdom is the function of the expositor, who draws not only from his study of scripture but from the many insights and*

108

interpretations of commentators and other Bible scholars."

Do you see what he has just done? That isn't a gift from the Spirit, it is rather, one's own ability to study well and have a good collection of commentaries to draw from. He misses the whole "of the Spirit" part of the gift. I thought Paul told the whole church in Colossae to "Let the word of Christ dwell in you richly as you teach and admonish with all wisdom" (Colossians 3:16), not just the Pastor.

He further says about the Gift of the Word of Wisdom, *"It is also the ability a counselor must have in order to apply God's truth to the questions and problems brought to him."* Where is the "revelation" part which the apostolic age operated in? Gone. Void. No longer works that way. John completely reinvents the definition of this gift, as he does Word of Knowledge, and Prophecy.

John, and many of those from the Cessationists camp, are incorrect about the function of the Gifts just as they are about the Gifts ceasing.

Remember I said that at times more than one Gift can be in operation. For example, a message in Tongues must be used with the Interpretation of Tongues following. Another example of both Gifts working at the same time is found in Matthew 17:24-27.

Jesus and his disciples arrived back in Capernaum, the town where Jesus was staying, very likely at the home of Peter and his wife and family. Every year, each male 20 years old or more had to pay the temple tax of two drachmas (about two days of wages) for the upkeep of the temple.

Peter was approached by those who collected the tax and was asked if he and Jesus were going to pay the tax. Peter said "yes" but didn't give them the money at that time. When Peter came into the house where Jesus was, Jesus spoke first and said, "What do you think Simon (Peter). From whom do the kings of the earth collect duty and taxes – from their own sons or from others?" "From others," Peter answered. (How did Jesus know this conversation had even happened? A Word of Knowledge).

Then Jesus proceeded to tell Peter what to do to pay the tax. Jesus said, "Go to the lake and throw out your line. Take the first fish you catch (Word of Wisdom); open its mouth and you will find a four – drachma coin (Word of Knowledge). Take it and give it to them for your tax and mine."

Are you getting it yet? These are things the Spirit knows and then reveals to God's people to use for direction, correction, encouragement and even warning. This is not common knowledge or wisdom gained from extra reading or study to figure things out; this is all from the Spirit of God. These gifts still work today.

Another example is found in Acts chapter 8. Philip, an evangelist in the early church, was holding an outstanding revival in Samaria. Multitudes were coming to salvation through faith in Jesus Christ, and God was enabling Philip to operate in the gifts of healings and miracles. The crowds were growing, the excitement was high, and I'm sure the money was rolling in. This is what all evangelists want. This was the kind of revival that can go on for weeks and months.

But all of a sudden, the Spirit of God tells Philip to leave this revival and go down to a desert road alone, in the middle of the day when it is hot, and wait for instructions. I'm sure Philip wanted to argue with God on this one. Leave a revival with multitudes attending and miracles happening to go down to a desert road alone in the middle of nowhere? But why, God?

God was giving him a Word of Wisdom, a "what to do next," which he would have never done on his own.

And of course, God had a reason; there was one man who would be traveling down that road at just the right time and God needed Philip to meet him and explain the way of salvation to him. And guess what, an Ethiopian eunuch, who was probably on his way back from Jerusalem and was reading a copy of the prophet Isaiah, was about to meet the evangelist.

The eunuch was reading the portion of scripture which talked about Jesus' suffering, but the eunuch wasn't able to understand who Isaiah was talking about. He needed someone who understood the Word of God and that is why God sent Philip there. Philip had literally left the ninety-nine and went to get the one!

So again, the Word of Wisdom is directional, and the Word of Knowledge is informational. But it only comes as the Holy Spirit reveals it and only when He wants to reveal it. I hope this is clear to you now.

CHAPTER 7

LET'S TALK ABOUT TONGUES

Next to Prophecy, or maybe even more than Prophecy, the most misunderstood of the nine Gifts of the Spirit is the issue of tongues, what Gordon Fee in his book, "God's Empowering Presence" called the "**Problem Child**" of the nine gifts, both as to the validity of tongues and their purpose. I believe one of the reasons so many non-Charismatics have a problem with this gift is due to the fact that we cannot understand a language that we don't understand. Do you understand? I am sure I can bring clarity to this topic by way of scripture and a little common sense.

In 2005, the Southern Baptist Convention (SBC) put out a statement disqualifying any new missionaries who filled out an application stating they practice speaking in tongues. In addition, if any existing members admitted to this practice of speaking in tongues, they were immediately disbarred.

However, on May 13, 2015, they rescinded that statement and are now accepting as part of their policy missionaries who are using a private prayer language, according to an article in Charisma news, dated 5/15/2015. Why this not-so-sudden change in policy?

The very nature of tongues is that it is foreign to both the speaker and the hearer. I honestly don't know why God chose this method of "not being able to communicate" as a way to communicate with us, and us with Him. That is, other than that it is a supernatural ability from the Holy Spirit, which when properly used, is beneficial to the individual and to the entire church family.

Paul said, "Undoubtedly there are all sorts of languages in the world, yet none of them is without meaning" (1 Corinthians 14:10). Meaning, all the languages in the world, and even angelic ones (see 1 Corinthians 13:1), are means of communication, whether you understand them or not.

I will be the first to admit that some of the tongues I have heard spoken by people do not sound like a human language. However, that would imply that I know every human language that is spoken, and I assure you that I don't. Have you ever heard an angel speak in their native language? What might that sound like? And what language does God speak when He communicates with the other persons of the Trinity or the angelic host? Remember, Jesus said in John 16:13, "But when he, the Spirit of truth, comes, he will guide you into all truth. He will not speak on his own; he will speak only what he hears, and he will tell you what is yet to come."

What language does the Holy Spirit hear from the Father? According to Romans 8:26, Paul said, "In the same way, the Spirit helps us in our weakness. We do not know what we are to pray for, but the Spirit himself intercedes for us with GROANS that words cannot express." Wow! What kind of language is that? Groans, that words cannot express? You tell me…

Paul continues in verse 27, "And he who searches our hearts knows the mind of the Spirit, because the Spirit intercedes for the saints in accordance with God's will." Can you imagine that communication between the Spirit and the Father? I have no idea what that must sound like. Groanings?

And Jesus also said, "For I did not speak of my own accord, but the Father who sent me commanded me what to say and how to say it. I know that his command leads to eternal life. So whatever I say is just what the Father has told me to say" (John 12:49-50). In what language did the Father speak to Jesus? Groanings? I believe Dr. MacArthur calls that "inter-trinitarian communication" (see his commentary on Romans 8).

We only have the explicit mention of tongues spoken in two books in the New Testament and a couple of implicit comments from the Old. In the New Testament we only find them mentioned in the book of Acts and 1 Corinthians. In the book of Acts we are told of the coming of the Gift of the Father, the Holy Spirit, which came on the day of Pentecost where they were all filled with the Holy Spirit and began to speak in tongues (languages) as the Spirit gave them utterance (Acts 2:1-4).

This is something completely different from the tongues mentioned in 1 Corinthians 12 and 14. Therein lies the confusion. Acts does not tell us how the Gift of Tongues and the Gift of Interpretation are to operate in the church, but rather, that they, along with Prophecy (see Acts 19:6), were the initial signs that the age of the Holy Spirit had arrived.

To understand how the Gift of Tongues (again, languages) should operate in the local church assembly, we must look to 1 Corinthians. Because Bible teachers try to teach them as one and the same, the confusion ensues. But if we separate the two examples, Acts and 1Corinthians, things become quite unequivocal rather quickly. That is, provided we believe they even exist at all in the church today.

What we do know for a fact, is, that Tongues were a part of the early church, and like Prophecy, not just for the apostles. Paul was writing to the CHURCH at Corinth, not other apostles. He was writing to Christians just like you and me. This was and is a genuine gift given by the Holy Spirit to believers who make up the Body of Christ. Tongues in 1 Corinthians have a purpose, but a purpose completely different from the tongues mentioned in the Book of Acts.

For example, nowhere in Acts do we see the Gift of Tongues with the Interpretation of Tongues mentioned. We only hear of and see the response of those who were filled with the Holy Spirit in Acts speaking in tongues as a sign that those who believed in the Lord Jesus Christ had received it. This happens in Acts 2, 9, and 19. It also seems to have happened in Acts 8 with Philip in Samaria, however, in that passage it does not explicitly say that the believers spoke in tongues; it is only implied.

Yet, most Bible scholars and teachers agree that in Acts 8 they must have spoken in tongues because it says when Simon SAW that the gift was given through the laying on of the apostles hands, he desired to be able to do what Peter and John had done; lay his hands on people whereby they would receive this gift. He saw something that was manifested when the apostles laid their hands on the people, and again most scholars are in agreement that what he saw was people speaking in tongues.

It can also be argued that in Acts 9, when Ananias laid his hands on Paul and told him to receive the Holy

Spirit, that he, Paul, must have spoken in tongues too. Why do I say that? Because the sign when someone had received the Holy Spirit in Acts was that they spoke in tongues. We know that Paul did speak in tongues because in 1 Corinthians 14, he said, "I thank God that I speak in tongues more than you all" (1 Corinthians 14:18).

If Paul did not receive tongues in Acts 9 through the laying on of Ananias' hands, when did he, and what would we call that? Did he simply have the Gift of Tongues? Maybe. But let me explain the difference in the two books, Acts and 1 Corinthians.

TONGUES IN ACTS

In Acts, the initial sign of the Spirit's coming (the gift the Father had promised), was the apostles speaking in languages they did not know and had never learned. Everyone agrees with this. This initial outpouring of the Spirit was made evident by the miracle of the 120 in the upper room speaking in these languages. There was no need for an "interpretation" of the tongues, for they were languages known "by those who heard them speaking the wonders of God in their own languages" (Acts 2:11). This was the sign to Israel that the Spirit had come upon the believing Jews as a sign to the unbelieving Jews.

So tongues in Acts 2 was a "sign" that the Spirit had now been given, just as the Father had promised. Again, in Acts 8 with Philip in Samaria, they spoke in tongues (presumably) but there was no need of interpretation because it was not a message, but rather a sign that Samaritans (half Jews) had received the Holy Spirit. Then again, in Acts 10 at Cornelius' house, they spoke in tongues and praised God. No need for an interpretation there either. Why? It was a sign that the Gentiles now had received the Gift of the Holy Spirit just like the Jews had in Acts 2.

Then once more in Acts 19, when Paul was in Ephesus, he laid hands on 12 disciples and they began to speak in tongues and also to prophesy. No need for interpretation here either. Why? Because it was a sign that they too had now received the Holy Spirit just like the Jews in Acts 2, and like the Gentiles in Acts 10. This is completely different than the purpose in 1 Corinthians, which I will explain in a moment.

So, what do we see so far; the Tongues spoken in Acts when they were filled with the Holy Spirit was a sign that the Holy Spirit had now been given and had filled each believer. Tongues was not the gift, the Holy Spirit was! Tongues was just the sign or the manifestation that they had received the Holy Spirit. It was also a sign to unbelieving Israel, which had, just like in the days of Isaiah, rejected their God (see Isaiah 28:7-12). It is sort of like circumcision. Circumcision wasn't the covenant, it was the SIGN of the covenant. Tongues was a sign that the Holy Spirit had come.

Please understand, these tongues or languages were unknown languages or tongues which the speakers did not know or had ever learned. It totally bypassed their intellect and was spoken through their mouths as the Spirit enabled them. Even though it was spoken fluidly and they were real languages, none of the speakers knew what they were saying. The hearers knew most of the languages but not all of them. Why do I say that? Because some thought they were drunk with new wine. Meaning, some of the languages they were speaking where in languages no one had heard before. Remember, there were 120 people doing this, including Mary, the mother of Jesus. Now let's look in the book of 1 Corinthians to see a different purpose for tongues.

TONGUES IN 1 CORINTHIANS

In 1 Corinthians, something completely different was happening. Although it was the same Holy Spirit, and the languages were foreign to the speakers, the purpose was not so much for a sign, but rather, it was a message from God which was to be interpreted so everyone could benefit. What I mean is, when a person genuinely spoke in Tongues in 1 Corinthians 12 and 14, they too were speaking as the Spirit enabled them, but for a completely different purpose. Let me explain.

In Acts, tongues were a sign that the Spirit had been given. It was spoken by believers who did not know what they were saying, but, at times, those present did. No need for an interpretation. In 1 Corinthians however, the Holy Spirit, the "gift giver," had enabled some believers to speak in a foreign language in a church setting as a message which had to be interpreted by another Gift of the Spirit, the Gift of the Interpretation of Tongues, so people would understand what God was trying to say.

In other words, the Gift of tongues was a Gift which neither the speaker nor the hearers understood and wouldn't do anybody any good unless it worked together with the gift of interpretation. Only when these two work together do they benefit anyone in the church. Because these two gifts are listed last in

121

Paul's lists in chapter 12 and 14, people have commented they are the least important. I believe Paul stated them last because these two are dependent on one another. By itself, the public gift of tongues doesn't do any good for the church. Interpretation of tongues wouldn't even happen without a tongue.

Yet, as Paul said, tongues with an interpretation is EQUAL to prophecy (1 Corinthians 14:5). Remember, prophecy is a gift of the Spirit in the known language of both the hearer and the speaker.

An example might be, if English is the language spoken in your church, and someone prophesied, that meant they stood up and spoke in English what they believe the Lord wanted to say, and both the hearers and the speaker could understand it perfectly, because it was in English.

A message in tongues, however, is a message in a foreign language which is foreign both to the speaker and the hearer. That is why Paul said if you have a message in tongues and there is no one to interpret it, either keep quiet and speak to God quietly or pray that you yourself get the interpretation (1 Corinthians 14:11-13, 27-28). This is not a TRANSLATION! It is NOT like someone stood up and spoke in Spanish and then someone else who understands Spanish translates what was spoken so the English-speaking people present could understand.

As we shall see in the next chapter, the interpretation of tongues is a supernatural Gift of the Holy Spirit to give a sense of what God is saying through the tongue which was spoken. Again, this is NOT a "word for word" translation.

After all, what is the context of 1 Corinthians 14? Paul is talking about using the Gifts of the Spirit to build up the body of Christ, the local church assembly. It was not for a "sign" that people had received the Holy Spirit. That was in Acts. In 1 Corinthians Tongues served to give instructions to the church. Paul wanted them to be wise in their use of tongues so as to benefit everyone by using whatever Gifts they had received to encourage the brothers and sisters in their local church. The only time Tongues and interpretation would be a "sign" is if there were unbelievers in the assembly that day (1 Corinthians 14:20-28).

This is why Paul said to "eagerly desire spiritual gifts" (1 Corinthians 14:1). Why? So the church would be edified, or built up (strengthened). The Holy Spirit gave all nine of these Gifts listed in 1 Corinthians 12 so that everyone could be part of a loving, growing, and encouraging church. But because of the abuse of Tongues, then and now, Cessationist leaders have found a way to discredit all Tongues today as phony and of no purpose.

I disagree with John here

For example, on his CD about tongues, which he taught at his church, entitled "The Simple, Surprising Truth about Tongues"(dated 2014, CD #44-7T), John states that there is no purpose for tongues today, that it was just for a 25 year span of time, and the purpose was for a sign to unbelieving Israel. He quotes Isaiah 28 because Paul makes mention of it in 1 Corinthians 14, and John turns his whole argument into a case about tongues only being a sign to show Israel that through the tongues of foreign people Israel would finally understand God's warnings as judgments to them. But remember, the church at Corinth was primarily a GENTILE CHURCH.

Isaiah was prophesying to a stubborn and rebellious nation, Israel, but that is not the argument Paul is making in 1 Corinthians. Paul was stating that tongues are for a sign to ALL unbelievers, Jew and Gentile, not just to the Jews, that God was truly speaking to them. Remember, Isaiah was talking about foreigners (the Babylonians) whose language Israel couldn't and wouldn't understand. There would be no interpretation following.

Again, Paul is setting the church in Corinth straight in their use of the Gifts, which they had turned into a circus. People were speaking out in tongues in church with no interpretation following, and it was only bringing confusion because obviously no one could understand what was being said. Most of the visitors at Corinth were Gentiles, not Jews. That is the context of 1 Corinthians 14.

TWO KINDS OF TONGUES IN 1 CORINTHIANS

In 1 Corinthians 14, there are two kinds of tongues listed, not counting the Gift of Interpretation of Tongues, or the tongues mentioned in the book of Acts. Let me explain.

We know that Paul listed nine different Gifts in 1 Corinthians 12, one of which is the Gift of Tongues. This is a public Gift which the Holy Spirit gives to whomever He wants. Not everyone has this public gift. The purpose, again, is to bring a message in a foreign language that neither the speaker nor the hearers understand. This Gift is totally dependent on another Gift, the Interpretation of Tongues. The two must work in tandem otherwise no one will benefit at all.

This is what the Corinthians were doing. People were standing up and speaking in foreign languages (whether or not they were always genuinely from the Holy Spirit is debatable) with no interpretation following, so no one received any encouragement or instruction at all. Sometimes there would be multiple messages given in Tongues without an Interpretation and it was bringing great confusion to the entire church.

This is why Paul wrote this chapter, to remind and instruct them of the purpose of Tongues, always to be followed by an Interpretation, which was to build up the body of Christ. Otherwise, they had missed the purpose of the Gift in the first place. People were getting "puffed-up" in pride over their Gift instead of being concerned about encouraging the whole church.

But Paul mentions another kind of Tongue, a private prayer language (tongues) which he wanted each believer to have. This was not for use in the church like the public Gift, which was to be followed by an Interpretation to build everyone up, but rather for the private use of each believer to build themselves up.

Paul says in 1 Corinthians 14:18, "I thank God that I speak in more tongues than all of you. But **in the**

church I would rather speak five intelligible words to instruct others than 10,000 words in a tongue." Why did he say that? Because the whole point of the passage is to build up the group!

Private prayer in Tongues only benefits the person praying. But when the church gathers, it is not for you the individual, but for the benefit of the whole group. **There is a place for speaking in Tongues without Interpretation, but the church is not it.**

The one caveat to this is, if the church, or house, or Bible study you are in does not have unbelievers or seekers present, and everyone present wanted to pray, sing, or worship in the Spirit (tongues), they certainly could do so.

Let me clarify something right here; A private prayer language, according to Paul in 1 Corinthians 14, does a couple of things. Paul says we are speaking mysteries, and thanking and praising God vss. 1-17. From our spirit, we are speaking to HIS SPIRIT though we do not know what we are saying to Him. It is, like all things, done by faith. Private Tongues for prayer is just that, private. This ability to pray in another language is given by the Holy Spirit who lives in every believer at the point of conversion. He graces us with this ability to speak by the Spirit, praise, thanksgiving, mysteries, and intercession. It is for the distinct purpose of building up the individual, not the body.

127

Listen to what the late Dr. Jerry Cook says in his book on the Holy Spirit entitled, "The Holy Spirit; So...what's the Big Deal?": *"Speaking in tongues must be de-mystified. In reality, these heavenly languages demand no more emotion than texting on your smartphone. They are not validated by volume, tears, shaking or swooning. Emotionalized, hysterical behavior is not of the Holy Spirit. We are talking about language, not behavior. We must not confuse the two. When we understand that we are talking about language the conversation becomes much simpler. Paul makes it very clear... He also explains that the Holy Spirit is able to give us a language by which we can speak directly and privately to God...It is spirit to God communication."*

Jude, the Lord's brother, who was probably among the 120 in the upper room on the day of Pentecost, wrote in his one chapter epistle in the book of Jude, "But you, dear friends, build YOURSELVES up in your most holy faith and pray in the Holy Spirit" (v20). All these leaders in the early church were Pentecostals and Charismatics. They all spoke in Tongues and taught the churches to do the same. Dr. MacArthur and others try to say that Jude is not referring to Tongues in this passage. But they have to say that because they don't believe Tongues are still available to the church. With that backdrop, what else can they say?

But Jude's language in that passage is almost identical to Paul's in 1 Corinthians 14:4, "Anyone who speaks in a tongue edifies themselves..." Edify and build up are the same thing! It is praying by faith in the Spirit and building yourself up.

Later, Paul says in Ephesians 6:18, "And pray **in the Spirit** on all occasions with all kinds of prayers and requests." I know Cessationists refuse to acknowledge this point because they have to, otherwise they would have to change their theology about it. But this is almost the same wording Paul uses in 1 Corinthians 14:14, where he says: "For if I pray in a tongue, **my spirit prays**, but my mind is unfruitful." Please understand, that Tongues by-passes our intellect because it is done by the Spirit in us. Paul continues, "So what shall I do? I will pray with **my spirit**, but I will also pray with my mind (my known language where my brain is involved); I will sing with **my spirit**, but I will also sing with my mind." I hope this is becoming clearer to you. You may not agree with it or even like it, but you can't deny that this is what it says.

Some people want to know if the person bringing the message in Tongues is also allowed or able to bring the interpretation? The answer is given by Paul himself in chapter 14:13, "For this reason anyone who speaks in a tongue should pray that he may interpret what he says." In other words, if someone has the public Gift of Tongues but there is no one there with the Gift of Interpretation, the person should pray and ask God for the Interpretation, otherwise they are to only pray quietly and speak to God.

So, what have we seen so far? Tongues in Acts were languages unknown to the speaker and a sign to those who heard it that the speaker had received the Holy Spirit, in part as a sign to unbelieving Israel. In those cases in Acts where it is mentioned, the **hearers** were able to understand their own language being spoken, even though the speakers did not know what they were saying and had never been taught the language they were speaking. So then, tongues was a sign that the Holy Spirit had now arrived.

In no case in Acts do we see the Gift of Interpretation of Tongues because the purpose of tongues in Acts was not a message to be translated, but rather a sign both of the filling of the Holy Spirit and to unfaithful Israel. However, I do want to make another point here: Peter had explained on the day of Pentecost that everyone who repented and believed on the Lord Jesus Christ would receive the gift of the Holy Spirit (Acts 2:38). What would be the sign that they had?

Answer: Speaking in other tongues, and in Acts 19, also prophesying. Remember Joel's prophecy? "In the last days I will pour out my Spirit on all people. Your sons and daughters will prophesy..." (Joel 2:28). Peter said, "This is that"...

My point is, every person, beginning in Acts 2 onward, who believed in Jesus Christ was to receive this gift called the Holy Spirit. My question is, did they all manifest the same sign as they did in Acts 2,8,10 and 19 of speaking in tongues? The scriptures are silent concerning this question. However, if the new believers didn't somehow reveal that they had received the Holy Spirit along with salvation, how would one know if they did? We know Paul said in Romans 8:9, "If any man has not the Spirit of Christ, he does not belong to Christ." But, at least in the book of Acts it seems the tell-tale sign they had received the Spirit was manifested by tongues and/or Prophecy.

But what about the churches in Galatia? Philippi? Berea? Thessalonica? Athens? We know the Corinthians did and so did the 12 disciples in Ephesus in Acts 19. But what about all the other saints in Ephesus who believed in Jesus while Paul stayed there for almost three years?

The scriptures seem silent, don't they?

Unless we add a couple of logical thoughts like, "why would Paul even ask the 12 disciples in Ephesus in Acts 19 if they had received the Holy Spirit if there was no way of telling?" I guess one could say that there seemed to be something deficient in their theology after talking with them for a while. That is plausible. But please remember this; when Paul arrived in Ephesus, it was 15 to 20 years after the day of Pentecost. What do I mean by that? Was the Holy

Spirit still manifesting His indwelling presence that many years later by believers speaking in other tongues, or had it been just isolated events?

If we can assume that the Holy Spirit still initially manifested his presence by enabling the believers to speak in tongues that many years later, can we not argue that ALL the other believers in those cities I just mentioned may also have spoken in tongues as an initial sign? I know, the scriptures seem to be silent.

We are often told not to argue from scripture's silence. But couldn't that work both ways? What I mean is, if the scriptures don't tell us whether the believers in those other cities (i.e. Philippi, Berea, etc.) spoke in tongues or not, can we argue the point either way, if the places in Acts 2,8,10 and 19 say they did? Don't those passages seem to state the norm of what happened rather than the passages that don't say either way being the norm? Something to think about.

Remember what Paul said in 1 Corinthians 4:16-17, "Therefore I urge you to imitate me. For this reason I am sending to you Timothy, my son whom I love, who is faithful in the Lord. He will remind you of my way of life in Christ Jesus, **WHICH AGREES WITH WHAT I TEACH EVERYWHERE IN EVERY CHURCH."** In other words, what Paul taught in one church he taught in all the churches.

Dr. MacArthur says in his commentary in 1 Corinthians and on his CDs on the Holy Spirit and Tongues, that the only time Paul mentions tongues is to the church at Corinth. Are we to seriously think that the church in Corinth was the only church to have the Gifts of the Spirit operating in it? Now that is a foolish argument from silence! What other letters in the New Testament besides the four Gospels and Acts talk about communion? Or about taking brothers to court or eating meat offered to idols? Do we then remove these issues from our theology because they are only mentioned in 1 Corinthians?

In fact, we do know that the churches (plural) in Galatia were operating in miracles and in the power of the Holy Spirit (see Galatians 3:5). But the issues Paul was addressing in those churches were different than the issues he was addressing to the Corinthians. The issues in the church at Corinth were because the Corinthians were acting so carnal in every aspect, especially when it came to the Gifts of the Spirit.

The Galatians were dealing with Judaizers who were teaching a "different gospel" than the pure gospel Paul had preached to them. Maybe they had a better handle on how the gifts were to properly function in the churches in Galatia. Paul did go back there a number of times to instruct and encourage them (Acts 14:21-23; 15:36, 41; 18:23).

THE REAPPEARING OF THE GIFTS OF TONGUES

In the late 1800's, in Topeka, Kansas, a man by the name of Charles Fox Parham began preaching a second outpouring of the Gift of the Holy Spirit and speaking in tongues. A few years later, the Azuza street revivals broke out under the ministry of William Seymore. Because the apostles in Acts 2 had to "wait" in Jerusalem for the Holy Spirit, Seymore and others thought that a person had to "tarry" (wait) for the Holy Spirit to come upon them.

Looking back, it isn't too difficult to see the error of their theology in thinking this way. They were wrong about the waiting, and they were wrong about how the tongues thing worked; they believed the languages would be known languages of the people they were to evangelize on the mission field. Yes, they were disappointed, big time.

They also didn't see the difference between tongues mentioned in the book of Acts and those mentioned in 1 Corinthians. They saw them as one and the same, for a "sign." But as I stated earlier, tongues in 1 Corinthians were for the edification or building up of the body when accompanied by the interpretation of tongues, but tongues in its private use is for the building up of the individual.

I want to state one more time: Tongues, the prayer language which I believe is available to every believer, can be used by any true Christian whenever they want.

That is why, again, Paul said, "I thank God I speak in tongues more than all of you." But the public Gift of Tongues is only given to those whom the Holy Spirit chooses to give it. Again, it must be followed by the Gift of Interpretation.

Think about this; if Paul told us to "eagerly desire spiritual gifts, and especially the gift of prophecy," and since the purpose of Prophecy is to encourage, comfort, and edify, that means God wants us to be encouraged, comforted, and edified. Wouldn't it make perfect sense then, that God would enable us to also do that for ourselves, as Paul says in 1 Corinthians 14:4, "He who speaks in a tongue EDIFIES HIMSELF, but he who prophesies, edifies the church." He then says in the next verse, "I would like every one of you to speak in tongues, but I would rather have you prophesy."

Now remember, the context of 1 Corinthians 14 is "how to build up the church body," it wasn't about Paul arguing against building up themselves. The people were abusing the purpose of the Gifts in the local church. The Gifts were "for the profit of all" (14:7). I hope this helps you understand the Gifts of Tongues better, both public and private.

CHAPTER 8

THE GIFT OF INTERPRETATION OF TONGUES

Because we covered the Gift of Tongues (the problem-child of the Gifts) rather extensively in the previous chapter, I will only cover the Interpretation of Tongues (the problem-child's companion) on what seems necessary to help us understand it gift better.

Interestingly, we have no examples of this gift in operation in the Bible. What we do have is an explanation of how this gift works, always along with the public Gift of Tongues first, as mentioned in the last chapter. It is only found in 1 Corinthians 12 and 14.

This Gift is valuable and does have great purpose when used properly in the church setting (it can also be used privately which I will tell you about as well). But let me begin with what it is not. It is NOT the human ability to understand a language that has been previously learned. For example, if you have the ability to speak both Spanish and English, and you were sitting in an English-speaking church, and someone stood up and gave a message in Spanish, and you interpreted what they said, IT WOULD NOT BE THE INTERPRETATION OF TONGUES.

Interpretation of tongues is a GIFT OF THE SPIRIT. It is not a known language that you simply interpret for those who don't understand. This is something the Holy Spirit enables some people to do as a Gift. It is supernatural. Remember, the Holy Spirit gives the Gifts as He chooses. However, all believers can pray for this Gift to operate in their life (1 Corinthians 14:13).

We would not know about this Gift had Paul not written to the church in Corinth and explained how it was to operate. Because he did, we have some understanding of how it works for us today. In 1 Corinthians 14, Paul straightens out the misuse and abuse of three Gifts in particular; Prophecy, Tongues, and the Interpretation of Tongues. Those are the only three Gifts he addresses in this chapter.

Why? They are the easiest ones to abuse. Paul said to eagerly desire the Gifts, but especially Prophecy. As I explained in the chapter on prophecy, prophecy is the gift spoken in the known language of both the speaker and the hearers. There is nothing supernatural about the language being spoken in prophecy, but rather, it is the message being delivered that is the work of the Spirit. The person is giving a "sense" of what God wants to say to the people who are present at the time.

It can be scripture, words of love, correction, or anything that doesn't violate God's Word. It can be something simple or profound.

Then Paul continues in that chapter by saying that "he who prophesies is greater than he who speaks in tongues, **UNLESS HE INTERPRETS**, so the church may be edified" (verse 5). In other words, prophecy, and tongues with an interpretation are equal, or equally valuable! I know that may shake up your theology a bit, but that is the Word of God, no matter what you have been told before.

Again, the context of 1 Corinthians 14 is the proper use of the Gifts and their purpose, which is building up the body of Christ. All the Gifts do that, when properly functioning in love, but the most prolific ones then and now are Prophecy, Tongues and Interpretation of tongues.

When a person brings a message in a language they have never learned (a Gift of the Spirit called Tongues), and someone interprets it (though they don't what language they are speaking nor do they understand it), they are giving a sense of what they believe the Spirit of God is trying to say to the congregation. Because it is only a "sense" of what they believe God is saying, what they say must be weighed (judged) by everyone who is there. Was it

139

Biblical? Did it make sense? Did it comfort, encourage, or edify? This is the test for whether or not the interpretation was from God.

When a Christian brings a message in tongues at the appropriate time in a service, but they are not sure if anyone has the Gift of Interpretation, they are either to keep quiet (vs. 28), or pray that they themselves may interpret what they said. Notice he said "pray that he may interpret". In other words, ask God to reveal to him (or her) what is the message to give to the body (church). If it was a known language, you wouldn't need to pray about it. But the fact that you need to pray and ask God proves this isn't something natural.

What the Cessationists have done is to get rid of all the Gifts because they have seen or heard of the abuses concerning them. But they also don't believe that tongues are actually languages like they were in Paul's day. Because these two Gifts go beyond the intellect, many have created a theology that says they no longer exist. That is really sad when Paul wanted everyone to prophesy and speak in tongues.

Paul's closing comment in chapter 14:39 is "Therefore, my brothers, be eager to prophesy, and do not forbid speaking in tongues. But everything should be done in a fitting and orderly way."

140

So, tongues are a Gift of the Spirit spoken in a language the speaker and the hearers do not know or understand. Interpretation of Tongues is a Gift given by the Holy Spirit to give a sense of what God said in the unknown language by someone who didn't understand it either. The Spirit of God gave them the sense of the meaning to communicate in the known language of the hearers for instruction, comfort, edification, or encouragement. Why did God choose these two Gifts to speak to His people in a local assembly instead of just communicating to them in the known language of the people, is a good question. Nevertheless, He did.

CHAPTER 9

THE GIFTS OF HEALINGS AND MIRACLES

In Dr. MacArthur's commentary on 1 Corinthians, he makes the following statement: *"The temporary sign gifts were limited to the apostolic age and therefore ceased after that time. These gifts included miracles, healing, languages, and the interpretation of languages. The purpose of the temporary sign gifts was to authenticate the apostolic message as the Word of God, until the time when the scriptures, His written Word, were completed and became self authenticating"* (pages 297-298).

Nowhere can Dr. MacArthur prove this from any scripture in the Bible. Again, who was Paul writing to? The church in Corinth. The Gifts were for the church, so everyone could profit by them. It is highly likely that at the time of Paul's writing to this church, there wasn't even an apostle present with them! These gifts were not ONLY to authenticate the preaching of the gospel, but also to heal sick people in their midst, to show the mighty deeds of God through a miracle whenever God deemed it necessary, and to speak words of encouragement through Tongues and

Interpretation when God wanted to them to know something specific.

Martin Luther, in his work "Letters of Spiritual Council" wrote the following:

"The tax collector in Torgau and the councillor in Belgern have written me to ask that I offer some good advice and help for Mrs. John Korner's afflicted husband. I know of no worldly help to give. If the physicians are at a loss to find a remedy, you may be sure that it is not a case of ordinary melancholy. It must, rather, be an affliction that comes from the devil, and this must be counteracted by the power of Christ with the prayer of faith. This is what we do and what we have been accustomed to do, for a cabinet maker here was similarly afflicted with madness and we cured him by prayer in Christ's name.

Accordingly you should proceed as follows: Go to him with the deacon and two or three good men. Confident that you, as pastor of the place, are clothed with the authority of the ministerial office, lay your hands upon him and say, "Peace be with you, dear brother, from God our Father and from our Lord Jesus Christ." Thereupon repeat the Creed and the Lord's Prayer over him in a clear voice, and close with these words: "O God, almighty Father, who hast told us through thy Son, verily, verily I say unto you, Whatsoever ye shall ask the Father in my name, he will give it you'; who hast commanded and encouraged us to pray in his

*name, 'Ask, and ye shall receive;' and who in like
manner hast said, 'Call upon me in the day of trouble:
I will deliver thee, and thou shalt glorify me;' we
unworthy sinners, relying on these thy words and
commands, pray for thy mercy with such faith as we
can muster. Graciously deign to free this man from all
evil, and put to nought the work that Satan done in
him, to the honour of thy name and the strengthening
of the faith of believers; through the same Jesus
Christ, thy Son, our Lord, who liveth and reigneth with
thee, world without end. Amen" Then when you
depart, lay your hands upon the man again and say,
"These signs shall follow them that believe they shall
lay hands on the sick, and they shall recover."*

*Do this three times, once on each of three successive
days. Meanwhile let prayers be' said from the chancel
of the church, publicly, until God hears them. In so far
as we are able, we shall at the same time unite our
faithful prayers and petitions to the Lord with yours.*

Farewell, Other counsel than this I do not have."

(- Tappert, ed., Luther: Letters of Spiritual Counsel,
nd. 18:52, Ch.1, p.52).

Dr. MacArthur randomly picks out these four Gifts,
with no proof whatsoever, based not on scripture, but
on selective choosings on his part from human
experiences or the lack thereof. I say selective
choosings, meaning John mentions church history

144

from situations when the church wasn't mightily operating in these Gifts. But he also selectively leaves out the many places where they were being practiced by men like Luther and Wesley.

Again I quote from Dr. Walter Martin's CD #3022, in which he states, **"Many people have operated in the Gifts of Healings and I have documented these healings in my latest book, '20th Century Pentecost' in which I have cataloged and verified these healings myself."** I do not know Dr. Martin to be a Pentecostal or a liar, nor would he put his name on the line for pseudo or false faith healers. Yet, he personally verified many healings in the 20th century and listed them in his book.

But let's see what the Bible says

Luke, the author of the book of Acts, was writing to a man named Theophilus. Most likely Theophilus was at one time (at least at Luke's first writing to him in the gospel of Luke) a high ranking official in the Roman army. He may have lost his position in the army due to his becoming a Christian, because Luke, at this second writing in Acts, does not address him as

"Most Excellent Theophilus," but rather simply as Theophilus. Why was Luke writing this account about Christians and Christianity to him?

One could not deny that he was showing him the growth of the Christian church as well as the working of the Holy Spirit through the Apostles AND OTHER CHRISTIANS in that first century. Luke chose specific things to write and tell Theophilus as the Holy Spirit led him to write them, in order for Theophilus to see how Christians were to live and what to believe. For example, in Acts 4:12, he quotes Peter as saying, "Salvation is found in no one else, for there is no other name under heaven given to men by which they must be saved" (talking about Jesus, of course). Luke was teaching Theophilus Christian doctrine.

He also spoke about the death of Jesus, the burial of Jesus, and the resurrection of Jesus. Not to mention the exaltation and return of Jesus too. But he also taught Theophilus about the operation of the Gifts of the Spirit all through the book of Acts. Would he do that only to then say, "Oh but they are not for you today." You can read about them but you can NEVER operate in them. It was only for then, not now." Why would God do that when we fight the same devil, deal with the same diseases, struggle with the same sins, battle the same discouragements, and face the same temptations?

The manifestations of the Spirit are given for the common good, or for the profit of each person in the church. Why would God only give them to the church at Corinth for just a little while and then do away with them? Does that even make sense? I think not. It was not, as John MacArthur says in his commentary on 1 Corinthians, to only authenticate the apostles' teaching and the gospel. Rather, these Gifts were given to the church so that they could profit as the body of Christ.

WHY DID JESUS DO MIRACLES?

Jesus didn't do miracles JUST to authenticate His ministry. The Word of God says that Jesus, "When he saw the crowds, had COMPASSION on them because they were harassed and helpless like sheep without a shepherd" (Matt 9:35-37).

Then again in Matt 14:14, "And Jesus went forth, and saw a great multitude, and was moved with COMPASSION toward them, and he healed their sick (KJV). And again in Matt 15:32, "Then Jesus called his disciples unto him, and said, 'I have COMPASSION on the multitude…'" (KJV).

One more time in Matthew 20:34, "So Jesus had COMPASSION on them, and touched their eyes: and immediately their eyes received sight…" (KJV). You can find this same reasoning of Jesus in Mark 1:41, 5:19, 6:34, 8:2, 9:22, Luke 7:13. In other words, Jesus healed and forgave because his heart was moved towards them because they were human and under the affliction of life and the assault of the devil, not just to show that He was God. In fact, Jesus was showing us the heart of God the Father, doing what the Father had both told Him to do and shown Him to do.

Remember why He healed the sick? He was showing us the heart of the Father. Jesus said, "If you have seen me you have seen the Father" (John 14:9-10). What did He mean by that? Jesus was saying that the works which I do are exactly what the Father would do. This is His (the Father's) will. Yes, I know God doesn't heal everyone but I know He wants to heal more than are being healed. The Kingdom of God is at hand! In other words, it is as close as your hand!

The miracles of Jesus were demonstrating what God's kingdom was all about; "To destroy the work of Satan," it says in 1 John 3:8. In Acts 10:38 it says "How God anointed Jesus of Nazareth with the Holy Spirit AND power, and how he went around doing good and HEALING all who were under the power of the devil, because God was with him."

Of course the miracles also demonstrated that He was from God and that He was the very Son of God, without question. Yes the miracles confirmed Jesus as the true Lord of heaven and earth, having been sent by the Father to prove His authority and to show us the heart of God towards humanity. But that is not the only reason. He was moved in His heart with compassion for a lost and dying world. That is why when He came in the words of Isaiah the prophet saying, "The Spirit of the sovereign Lord is upon me, for he has anointed me to preach good news to the poor. He has sent me to proclaim freedom for the prisoners and recovery of sight for the blind, to release the oppressed, to proclaim the year of the Lord's favor" (Luke 4:18-19).

No, not everyone gets healed. We all get sick sometimes, and we will all certainly die (unless Jesus comes back first); the death rate is still one per person. GOD DOES NOT HEAL EVERYONE. Neither did Jesus. He healed almost no one in his hometown of Nazareth (Mark 6:1-6). Jesus only healed one out of a "great number" who were sitting at the pool of Bethesda (John 5:1-15). We know Jesus walked by the man at the gate Beautiful many times and never offered to heal him until the disciples did in Acts 3:1-10. There are many more I can list. But the point is, God did heal, does heal, and wants to heal more than He does, but when you have Christian leaders who are telling you the Gifts are not for us today, it's pretty tough to have faith.

Think about it; would you rather go to a Word of Faith church, or a Word of Doubt church? Now, you know I am being facetious. But you get the point. I know that some of the things which are and have been spoken in the Word of Faith church are out in left field, and some have left the ballpark all together! But to swing the bat all the way to the other side of the field, where the church has no faith at all, isn't any good either.

Wasn't it Jesus who said, "However, when the Son of Man comes, will he find faith on the earth?" (Luke 18:8). How many times did Jesus say "Oh ye of little faith?" And He was talking to the disciples who had seen His miracles on a regular basis. How could they have doubted? Because it is our human nature to be skeptical. When we were children we were gullible. We believed almost anything anyone told us. But as we became older, we started to learn that not everyone could be trusted, including, at times, even our parents. They made mistakes too.

So in the church, because many so-called "Charismatics" have said some foolish things and have deceived gullible people, as John MacArthur so eloquently referenced in his book, we have become skeptical of the whole "GIFTS THING." But being skeptical doesn't equal being Biblical!

So if Jesus only did what He saw His Father doing (John 5:19-20), then that must mean whatever Jesus did is just what the Father told Him and showed Him to do. That is what the Father's will is, to destroy the works of Satan. Which leads us to the next question: What are the works of Satan? Poverty? Disease? Sickness? Sin? Lies? Deception? False doctrine? A religious spirit? Pride? Remember, "The thief comes only to steal and kill and destroy" (John 10:10). Jesus came that we might have life more abundantly! So if Satan is behind all these things in the hearts and minds of men, God sent His son not only to die as the payment for our sins, but also to establish God's kingdom back on this planet. Is that not what Jesus did?

I am not spouting a "name it and claim" it Word of Faith theology here. I am reminding the church that Jesus didn't do miracles to just authenticate his ministry. He also did them because the Father loves us so desperately, and Jesus was moved with compassion towards the people to heal them and set them free because that is the heart of the Father.

Again in Luke 4, Jesus came into His hometown of Nazareth and went as was His custom into the synagogue. He was handed a scroll, or a copy of the Old Testament. He stood up and found the place in Isaiah where it says, "The Spirit of the Lord is on me, because he has anointed me to preach good news to the poor. He has sent me to proclaim freedom for the prisoners and recovery of sight for the blind, to release the oppressed, to proclaim the year of the Lord's favor" (Isaiah 61:1). Now if Jesus came to destroy the works of the devil and to heal all who were under the power of the devil, then we have a pretty good picture of what the works and power of the devil are.

We know Satan harasses people and makes them believe they are helpless or deceives them into thinking they don't need help. We know that he oppresses people, binds them in all kinds of prisons of addictions and behaviors and negative and sinful patterns of thinking. We know he blinds the eyes of men both spiritually and physically. We know that Satan did not want men to know the truth of God's word or what Jesus called "God's favor," which had now arrived. So Jesus came bringing the kingdom and healing everywhere He went.

The miracles absolutely did authenticate His ministry and His person, but they did far more than that. They healed, set free, and revived people whom the devil had harassed for ages. After Jesus ascended back to the Father, He saw to it that we would have the same Spirit which He had; God's Holy Spirit. The Apostles were the first ones to receive the Spirit, but not the only ones. Peter said, "The gift is for you and for your children, for those who are far off. For as many as the Lord our God shall call" (Acts 2:38).

Even Peter didn't understand the scope of what he was saying at the time. He believed this "Gift" was only for the far-off Jews. Just think, Peter with a deficient theology. Amazing. The Lord had to command Peter to go to the Gentiles in Acts 10, because Peter hadn't yet understood the magnitude of God's love for ALL NATIONS.

So now the Apostles begin acting like Jesus, their Lord, with miracles, signs, and wonders. But it wasn't just for them. In Luke 10 we see 70 other men (disciples) whom Jesus gave power and authority to go out and preach the full gospel; "Heal the sick who are there and tell them the kingdom of God is near you " (Luke 10:9). Then later on after Jesus' resurrection and ascension in Acts 6, we come across some Jews who were not raised in a Hebrew synagogue and did not speak the Hebrew language.. Rather, they were Greek speaking Jews who loved Jesus and submitted to the leadership of the Jerusalem church.

Stephen and Philip are the first two. Both these men walked by faith and in the power of the Holy Spirit. "Stephen, a man full of God's grace AND power, did great wonders and miraculous signs among the people" (Acts 6:8). Say what you want but these men were not Apostles! Stephen was only a lay-leader in the church, and he did these miracles not only to authenticate the gospel, but because people's lives were being destroyed by Satan. God is for the people, not against them.

Philip is the next one on the scene. In Acts 8, Philip preaches in Samaria and he too was a man full of faith AND power. He too did miraculous signs in front of and for the people. Why were these men able to do these wonderful things? One reason is because Jesus their Lord had done them first. By the way, did I mention that Jesus was a Charismatic? After He ascended, The Father and Jesus sent the Holy Spirit so that we would receive that same power our Lord had.

Another reason they were enabled to do these things is because healings and miracles are from the very heart of God. To heal, set free, and deliver is God working through us. God has compassion for people. I mean why else would you pray for a sick person if you didn't think God wanted to heal them? If you believe God doesn't want to heal them, then why even pray for the sick? God healed and delivered and set free all the way to the end of the book of Acts. Even in the last chapter of the book, chapter 28, Paul is still healing people on the Island of Malta. Not just to authenticate the gospel, but because people were sick!

A miracle as defined by Webster is 1) an extraordinary event manifesting divine intervention in human affairs;

2) an extremely outstanding or unusual event, thing, or accomplishment.

Miracles are as much a part of the Bible narrations as the teachings and healings are. From Sarah having a child at 90 years old, to Moses parting the Red Sea, to the walls of Jericho coming down, to Jesus walking on water, to calming a storm, to raising Lazarus from the dead, to miracles taking place in the Galatian churches (Gal 3:5). The list goes on and on.

God gives supernatural ability to people He chooses to do these things at specific times in specific situations. Nowhere does it say that miracles stopped. Nowhere. Can you quote me one scripture that says they have stopped? Just one? Nope, not even one. But who among us believes they can still happen? If we don't believe it can happen, then it won't!

Healings are still alive today also. But who is asking God for this Gift today? Are you? Do you believe God still wants to use people and to have these Gifts today? If we are taught that they don't exist anymore, no wonder no one is asking for them and no wonder they aren't happening in your church. But we wouldn't even be arguing this point if Paul hadn't mentioned it in 1 Corinthians 12-14. We would just all believe it was only for the early church and the Apostles. But didn't the Galatian church operate in this gift too?

Paul said in Galatians 3:5, "Does God give you his Spirit and **work miracles** among you because you observe the law, or because you believe what you heard?" Remember, Paul wasn't talking to other Apostles. He was talking to ordinary believers just like you and me at a time when there were no Apostles present in the Galatian churches. Now it's up to you to believe, or not.

I know what you are thinking right now, "Then how come we don't see genuine miracles taking place today?" First of all, who says they aren't taking place? Let's begin with ministries in other countries like Africa, Latin America, and the Orient. There are endless testimonies, thousands upon thousands of them, of people being healed, raised from the dead and unbelievable situations turned around by God's power through people of faith.

However, whenever a non-charismatic hears about them, there is often instant speculation and cynicism on their part. They doubt the veracity of what is being reported. Why? Because they begin with the belief system which says they no longer happen. Shame on them! God is the God who calls things that are not as though they were (Romans 4:17). But how does God often do these things? Through His people whom He anoints and equips. We don't see nearly as much here in America because the church has lost its power and replaced it with programs. We have focused on teaching and have thrown out the doing (Acts 1:1). We have conferences for everything. How to control our anger, how not to lust after a woman, how to get over depression, understanding the book of Revelation, how to teach men to be men, conferences on worship, leadership, etc...

The list goes on and on.

But what about a conference about the power and presence of the Holy Spirit to bring healing to the sick, power to the weak, and faith to the doubting? And whenever a true Christian gets up and begins to preach these things, they get shot down with our own rifles. It has been said that Christians shoot their own wounded. We also dis-fellowship those who stand in great faith.

But read your New Testament; It is replete with healing after healing, and miracle after miracle. But who is paying the price in prayer? I don't mean our simple and sincere devotional life. I mean a consecrated life of seeking the face of God and not just His hand. We are so adept at asking God to meet our needs (which Jesus said the Father knows before we even ask), that we seldom fight for doing His will.

Paying the Price in Prayer

Earlier I told you the story of the Baptist pastor who I was talking with on the 2nd hole as I was playing with John MacArthur at his country club. When the pastor, Harry Walls, asked me "How does this happen in your church" (talking about healings in our services), I told him that for me it has required much more time in prayer. Seeking the face of God beyond our normal daily prayer times is the most important aspect of seeing God do amazing things in your life. But who is willing to pay the price to do this?

There is a story in Mark 9 of a demon possessed boy whom Jesus' disciples are trying to cast out but with no ability to do so (this story is also found in Matt 17 and Luke 9). Jesus, along with Peter, James, and John, had been on the mount of Transfiguration where Moses and Elijah met with Jesus discussing many things (see Mark 9:1-6).

As they were coming down the mountain, they were met by a crowd of people who arguing and Jesus wanted to know why. A man approached him and said, *"Teacher, I brought you my son, who is possessed by an evil spirit that has robbed him of speech. Whenever it seizes him, it throws him to the ground. He foams at the mouth, gnashes his teeth and becomes rigid. I asked your disciples to drive out the spirit, but they could not."*

"O unbelieving generation," Jesus replied, *"how long shall I stay with you? How long shall I put up with you? Bring the boy to me."* So they brought him. When the spirit saw Jesus, it immediately threw the boy into a convulsion. He fell to the ground and rolled around, foaming at the mouth. Jesus asked the boy's father, "How long has he been like this?"

"From childhood," he answered. It has often thrown him into fire or water to kill him. But if you can do anything, take pity on us and help us." "If you can?"

158

said Jesus. Everything is possible to him who believes." Immediately the boy's father exclaimed, "I do believe; help me overcome my unbelief!"

When Jesus saw that a crowd was running to the scene, he rebuked the evil spirit. "You deaf and mute spirit," he said, "I command you to come out of him and never enter him again." The spirit shrieked, convulsed him violently and came out. The boy looked so much like a corpse that many said, "He's dead." But Jesus took him by the hand and lifted him to his feet, and he stood up.

*After Jesus had gone indoors, his disciples asked him privately, "Why couldn't we drive it out?" He replied, "**THIS KIND** can only come out by prayer and fasting."* (Emphasis mine).

In looking at this story, I have to ask you, "What Kind?" What kind can only come out by prayer and fasting? And how much prayer and fasting? Why couldn't the other disciples cast the devil out of the boy? They had been successful in other places, why not here?

When Jesus asked the boy's father how long the boy had been like this, the father told us what kind; The kind that have been around a long time. "Since his childhood," the dad said. In other words, when demons have had access into our lives concerning addictions, sickness, improper ways of thinking, and diseases, for extended stays, the situation isn't going to simply change and they aren't coming out with a single prayer from the average Christian who only prays 10 minutes a day.

In serious life situations, Jesus said this kind is going away without people seeking the Lord in fasting and prayer. You have to be filled with the Holy Spirit's power in order to operate in healing Gifts and miracles. But who is paying the price and praying this way? Remember what Peter said in Acts 6, "We must give ourselves to PRAYER and the Word."

Again in Acts 4:29-31, Peter prayed and said, **"Now, Lord, consider their threats and enable your servants to speak your word with great boldness. Stretch out your hand to heal and perform miraculous signs and wonders through the name of your holy servant Jesus."** Who is praying like this anymore? But if you don't believe God still does these things, you won't pray this way. No wonder we don't see many healings and miracles, except in people and churches who dare to ask God for His power to be present in our lives.

If Jesus said, "I have come to do my Father's will," and God is immutable (unchanging), and Jesus Christ is the same yesterday and today and forever, and Jesus said "You shall receive POWER when the Holy Spirit comes upon you," shouldn't we ask God to enable us to do the things Jesus did? After all, didn't Jesus say we would do greater things than He did (John 14:12)?

160

What I am trying to say is, until we sincerely ask God for the precious Gifts of His Holy Spirit, as Paul said to do (1 Corinthians 14:1), can we really just say "they no longer exist for us today?" Teach we must and teach we will, but the same Bible which commands us to "Preach the Word" (2 Timothy 4:2), is the same Bible which says, "And these signs will accompany those who believe...and they will place their hands on sick people, and they will get well" (Mark 16:15-18).

Healing in the Bible was almost always dramatic and instantaneous. But not always. In Mark 8:22-23 Jesus laid his hands on a blind man to heal him, but it took Him two tries. There was a partial healing the first time and then a complete healing at the second touch of Jesus. And He is God! We who sometimes don't have enough faith to pray for a hangnail, have no faith for someone with cancer or diabetes. We simply say, "The Lord's will be done," or worse yet, "you're gonna die."

But let's move on to the next Gift, the Gift of Faith.

CHAPTER 10

THE GIFT OF FAITH

4 Different kinds of faith

There are four different kinds of faith that I will discuss with you now. Each of the first three have their own distinct value which will lead us to the fourth kind, the Gift of Faith.

The first one is what I will call natural faith. This is the faith that every human being operates in on a regular basis. This is faith to trust natural or man-made events or things which we all depend on. For example, we trust that when we pull up to the gas pump we believe that what is coming through the hose is actually gasoline that will not harm our vehicles. This is trust in man that the gasoline is gasoline.

When we cross a bridge, we trust that the bridge will not collapse. We have faith that when we step on the brakes of our car, the car will stop. Or how about the food we eat, especially at the restaurant. We have

faith that the food isn't poisonous and it won't kill us
or give us food poisoning. We have faith that the chair
at our neighbor's house or at the church house will
hold up our weight when we sit down.

This is everyday faith which we all utilize regularly.

The second kind of faith is "The Faith." This is the
gospel of Jesus Christ. This is the doctrine we hold to
that Jesus is Lord and is the only way to the Father.
We might ask someone if they are "in the faith." Paul
the Apostle said, "I have fought a good fight; I have
run the race and I have kept the faith" (2 Timothy 4:7).

In many communities around our country we have
gatherings of all the "communities of faith." This is an
ecumenical gathering of different religious groups
coming together for a specific cause or purpose. There
might be Hindus, Buddhists, Mormons, Muslims,
Christians, and Catholics in the same room. But when
I say "The Faith" I mean, people who hold to the
gospel of Jesus Christ. People who have believed in
their heart that God raised Him from the dead, and
have confessed with their mouth that Jesus is Lord.

 The third kind of faith is called "a measure of faith."
This is found in Romans 12:3, where Paul said "in
accordance with the measure of faith God has given
you." This means that once we accept "The Faith,"
God gives each believer a measure of faith to begin
their Christian walk. This faith in God is to live our

Christian life, trusting God in trials, for provisions, protection, healing, or whatever needs or situations a believer faces. Hebrews 11:6 says, "Without faith it is impossible to please God; those who come to him must believe that he is (God), and he is a rewarder of those who diligently seek him."

This faith is the kind of faith that is to increase and grow as you walk with the Lord as a way of life. It grows from reading the Word of God and grabbing on to His promises as you face trials of many kinds. It grows by thinking about the trials that God has already brought you through. You begin to realize more and more that God can be trusted and He will bring you through the difficulties you face, and with that, He also gives you a peace in the trial that goes beyond your ability to comprehend (Phil 4:6-8).

The fourth kind is called the Gift of Faith. This is a special endowment given to people whom the Holy Spirit chooses to have this supernatural faith. In my experience and theology, this Gift seems to work often in tandem with other Gifts, such as Miracles and Healings. In other words, the ability to do miracles or to heal people (although, in fact it is God doing the healing) is propelled by or has its impetus in the Gift of Faith working with these other Gifts.

It can also be that God gives you a supernatural confidence that even though the situation before you seems impossible and ominous, somehow you know it is all going to work out. You have a deep peace in the midst of the storm. Your words become faith-filled and others around you take notice that you are acting and speaking strangely different than other Christians.

Notice Dr. MacArthur's statement about this gift of Faith in his commentary on 1 Corinthians 12 on page 300; *"Countless missionaries have **claimed** tribes or nations for the Lord, and evangelists have **claimed** cities for the Lord, and seen him faithfully respond to their faith. Their prayers are answered and their faith itself is strengthened and multiplied"*. Wow! Almost sounds like John is from the "name it and claim" it church!

It is probable that this is the kind of faith which Stephen and Barnabas possessed as Luke described these men (Acts 6:8, 11:24). It is possible that this is what came over Peter to step out of the boat onto the water to join Jesus (Matt 14:22-29). I say it is possible, because it may also be possible that these men simply had learned to trust God. I will let you decide.

The Gift of Faith is a deeper level of knowing for certain that God is going to do what we ask of Him. "Now faith is the substance of things asked for; the evidence of things not seen" (Hebrews 11:1).

CHAPTER 11

DISCERNING OF SPIRITS

This Gift is highly valuable in the body of Christ today due to the proliferation of errant doctrine which comes into the church through men who are false teachers and people who attempt to deceive and prey upon believers.

"For such men are false apostles, deceitful workmen, masquerading as apostles of Christ. And no wonder, for Satan himself masquerades as an angel of light. It is not surprising, then, if his servants masquerade as servants of righteousness. Their end will be what their actions deserve" (2 Corinthians 11:13-15).

Paul makes it abundantly clear in this statement that workers of the devil himself will come into our assemblies and try to deceive people. Jude, in his epistle, states the same thing by saying, *"For certain men whose condemnation was written about long ago have secretly slipped in among you. They are godless men, who change the grace of our God into a license for immorality and deny Jesus Christ our only Sovereign and Lord"* (Jude 4).

How are we to combat these deceptive people? One of the ways God has provided for us is through the Gift of Discerning of Spirits. This is the ability to read through an individual's motives and intents and also realize the clandestine spirit which indwells them. They only mean to bring confusion and harm to the body of Christ. Their purpose is deception. They are led by Satan himself whether they themselves are aware of it or not.

Some Biblical examples might be Paul and his entourage in Acts 16 who daily went outside the city for prayer, due to the fact there wasn't a Jewish synagogue in Philippi. It required ten Jewish men in a city to constitute the building of a gathering place, or synagogue (which by the way, is what the word synagogue means). Since Philippi was a Roman colony and not a Jewish ghetto, there was no synagogue there. This was a city where Roman soldiers who had served Rome in their army were allowed to retire (whether they were Roman or not).

When Paul was directed by the Holy Spirit to go to Philippi and bring the gospel to the people, he went outside the city to find a quiet and peaceful place to pray with his companions. This is where he met Lydia and her female friends who had already gathered there. After Paul did his social protocol of introducing himself to these ladies, he preached Christ to them and they believed (Acts 16:11-15).

On one occasion, when Paul and his companions were going to prayer, they were met by a girl who had a spirit of divination. She had been empowered by a demon spirit to predict the future and her owners made quite a bit of money off her supernatural, albeit ungodly ability. After a few days of listening to her, Paul DISCERNED that Satan was behind this ability, and proceeded to cast the demon out of her.

She had been speaking a truth, that Paul was teaching the people the way to get saved through Jesus Christ. However, Paul was not about to let **her** validate **his** message. The reason being, if Paul let her go on saying this truth about him and his message, she could dupe the people into believing other things she would say could be trusted also.

Satan, who is the Father of lies, knows that every good liar always tells a little bit of truth, but never the whole truth. So when Paul discerned where her power originated from, he cast the demon out of her. Discerning of spirits enabled him to know this.

A very clear example of discerning of spirits, or in this case, a spirit, is the story in Luke 13 which I mentioned earlier, when Jesus identified the root issue behind the physical manifestation, Satan himself. In the story of the woman bent over in the synagogue whom Jesus called forward and then healed. Everyone thought she simply had a bad or deformed back, possibly scoliosis. But Jesus looked beyond the symptom to the one who had caused this condition. Satan. Jesus said "Should not this woman, a daughter of Abraham be loosed from what has bound her?" Satan was the one who had bound her and was holding her that way. No one else seemed to have realized this.

Another case in point is when Peter came down to Samaria as Philip was holding a revival there and many people were getting saved. Philip asked for the church leadership in Jerusalem to come down to Samaria and lay their hands on the new believers that they might receive the Holy Spirit. So they sent Peter and John as the representatives.

Unfortunately, there was a man there named Simon Magus who had deceived the people in that town for many years through the use of magic. This too was given him by demonic power for the distinct purpose of deceiving the people into thinking that he was some great power   (Acts 8:4-17).

When Simon Magus saw that Peter and John had this incredible ability to lay hands on people and they would begin speaking in other languages which they previously did not know, he too wanted this ability. In fact, he was willing to pay a lot of money to learn how to do this new "magic trick." However, Peter was able to discern that his heart and motive were not right and that he was still a captive of Satan, so Peter confronted him and set him straight.

In my experience with this gift of discerning of spirits, God seems to give believers a keen awareness of who people are and who they are serving, oftentimes by what they say or don't say. It seems, all of a sudden, you become acutely aware of their every word and how they phrase things, their facial expressions or their name-dropping of famous people, especially Christian leaders.

You have a strong sense that "something ain't right with this person." You find yourself probing them with deep questions, checking their belief in who Jesus is and asking them to clarify terms. Whenever you have this "check" in your spirit, it is best to trust it and be very cautious with this person.

Another case in scripture is where Paul had warned the Ephesian elders in Acts 20 to *"watch out for savage wolves who will come in among you and will not spare the flock. Even from your own number men will arise and distort the truth in order to draw away disciples after them"* (Acts 20:29-30).

These might be people who would sit in their assemblies on a Sunday morning, men, who as Jude said, would "secretly slip in among you." Peter said there would be false teachers among us (2 Peter 2:1). He continued, *"They will secretly introduce destructive heresies, even denying the sovereign Lord who bought them - bringing swift destruction on themselves. Many will follow their shameful ways and will bring the way of truth into disrepute"* (vss 2-3).

I have found that women, often have this ability to discern when someone is not right. I know this may at times simply be a "woman's intuition," but at other times, God is making her keenly aware of another person's purpose. Whenever a woman of standing in our church has warned me about a certain person who has started attending our church, I have learned the hard way to listen to them. This is especially true when it comes to other females. Men have a way of being duped by a pretty face, especially when she is cloaked in a nice personality or is complimentary. But other women sometimes have the ability to read right through this masquerade. Listen to them!

CHAPTER 12

THE CHURCH AT CORINTH

When Paul addressed the Corinthian church in Chapters 12-14, it was because he had learned that after he left the city, the church leadership had somehow allowed their public gatherings to become disorderly through a complete misuse of the Gifts which were meant to be valuable.

The problem wasn't with the Gifts and them not being needed or real, the problem was in the improper use of them. These carnal Christians in Corinth were using these Gifts haphazardly and in complete disorder. God made it clear that He is NOT a God of disorder, but of peace (1Cor 14:33). But please read the verse right before this one; "The spirits of the prophets are subject to the control of the prophets" (vs. 32). What does that mean? It means that each person has the ability to control or not control himself when the Spirit of God gives him/her something to share.

Unfortunately today, we have "thrown out the baby with the bathwater." If Paul would have taken the line of reasoning which many of our Cessationist brothers have taken, Paul would have said, "Alright, that's enough of this gift stuff. From now on, no more of this." But he didn't. Instead, and rightfully so, he wrote to remind or instruct them of the proper use of these Gifts and how they were to function in their public gathering times.

Let's look at it logically

For the Gifts of the Spirit to be in operation, He, the Holy Spirit, prompts or urges the individual to speak something (talking about the verbal gifts; i.e. prophecy, tongues, word of knowledge, word of wisdom, interpretation of tongues) to the church or an individual. It is at that moment each person can use the Gift or hold on to it, speak at the appropriate or wrong time or choose to be quiet. He is in control of his own spirit. That is why Paul says emphatically "do not quench the Spirit" (1 Thess 5:19). What does that imply? That you can quench the Holy Spirit. You and I actually have the ability to NOT let the Spirit use us.

Again, we also have the ability to speak up at the wrong or improper time in a service as proved by Paul in 1 Corinth 14: 27-28, "If anyone speaks in a tongue, two-or at the most three-should speak, one at a time, and someone must interpret. If there is no interpreter, the speaker should keep quiet in the church and speak to himself and God." In other words, keep control of yourself in church and do everything in order the way God says to. "The spirit of the prophet is subject to the prophet."

The Holy Spirit may indeed be giving you something to say (or do) but the Gift has to be used at the appropriate time and in the appropriate way. Yes, many have misused their Gifts given by God. Others may be ignorant about how and when to operate in these Gifts. That is not so hard to understand. Basically, on one hand, we are talking about church etiquette and on the other hand about accuracy of what is said and genuineness of what is being done.

How would a young believer ever learn how to operate in the Gifts if he didn't step out and use them? That is what Paul said in verse 31, "You can all prophesy in turn so that everyone may be instructed and encouraged." The fact that we are to "judge all things and hold on to that which is good" (1Thess 5:21), and "two or three prophets should speak, and the others should weigh carefully what is said" (1Cor 14:29), implies that not even in the early church was there "automatic acceptance" of everything said even among the prophets (or those who prophesied).

Why would they have to weigh carefully or judge all things every time someone spoke by the Spirit? I am sorry, like it or not, what is spoken from the Holy Spirit through a vessel **IS** more subjective than the written word. And please remember, the church in Corinth, or any other church for that matter in the first century, did not have the full written Word of God.

What criteria was used when judging whether a tongue or a prophecy was spoken? If they didn't have the Bible to reference what was said, they must have judged it by what Paul, Apollos, Peter, or any of the other leaders must have taught them.

And what about the fact that there were not Apostles and Prophets sitting in every church or in every service in the first century? That meant the elders and leaders who were spiritual and more mature were to be the judges of what was said and done in the churches. Their job (along with preaching and teaching and praying) was to

a) **Allow** freedom of the Spirit to operate, b) **Give direction** in the services as to what the Holy Spirit was saying or doing, c) **Pay attention** to what was being said, d) **Judge** the accuracy of what was said.

- a. Allow freedom
- b. Give direction
- c. Pay attention
- d. Judge

Dr. MacArthur continuously argues throughout his writings in commentaries and in his books, that the gifts of the Spirit and any new revelation supposedly deemed to have come from the Holy Spirit, are not true or valid because God doesn't do that anymore (see his commentaries on 1 Cor, Romans, and 1 Thessalonians; also his book Charismatic Chaos). He argues that church doctrine was built on the "foundation of the apostles and prophets, with Jesus Christ himself being the chief cornerstone" (Eph 2:19-20). Of course I agree with this verse completely. However, can you produce one document from a first century prophet written as the Word of God? Nope. Not even one.

Remember, the context of 1 Corinthians 14 is the proper use of tongues and prophecy. When I speak of the Gift of Prophecy, which again, Paul said he wanted each of us to eagerly ask for, I am not talking about **ADDING ANYTHING TO SCRIPTURE**. I am talking about thoughts, ideas, encouragements, corrections and even scripture, that the Holy Spirit is prompting us to share with one another.

Paul's attitude toward the Gifts in the church in Corinth wasn't, "Geez, I can't wait until that which is perfect comes so we won't have to deal with this "gift stuff" anymore." Rather, he was instructing them to use these precious Gifts in the way God had designed them to be used. It was never God's or Paul's intent to throw them out because they were being abused and misused. They are of great value to the body of Christ both then and now.

CHAPTER 13

PROOF THAT THE GIFTS HAVE NEVER CEASED

WHERE JOHN AND I AGREE AND DISAGREE

Dr. MacArthur, in lawyer like fashion, gives a litany of names and quotes in his book which would make almost any Christian say, "**They said what**?" C. Peter Wagner, Benny Hinn, and many others have said some very peculiar things about Christ, doctrine, and the Bible. I agree with John. (However, let me state here, John has quoted some questionable resources concerning these individuals which should be researched as to their accuracy).

The unfortunate part is, not only are the people John mentions classified as Charismatics, but it is quite shameful that Christians in general would say such things. It doesn't matter to me if they are Baptist, Lutheran, Presbyterian, or whatever other denomination they may be from. If they call themselves Christians they must be careful what they believe and teach. One thing I do want you to notice is that almost all of the people John mentions are independent people with independent ministries. In other words, they are not from a structured denomination with checks and balances. This is an important point to consider.

In the Foursquare denomination from which I come, we have a set of bylaws and doctrines that we have to adhere to. If we were found to be making heretical statements about Christ or the Bible, we would be warned, and if no change was forthcoming we would be removed. But when you have independent ministries with a "talking head" at the helm who answers to no one, you have more opportunity to get off track. The people John quotes, for the most part, are these kinds of leaders, independents with no one to question them. When someone does speak out, they become defensive and say that the person doesn't know what they are talking about. Again, I agree with John.

When John quotes Benny Hinn as saying "There are nine persons in the Godhead," Benny should be rebuked. (5) Or when Oral Roberts said if he didn't raise eight Million dollars for his hospital Jesus would take him home, again, foolish thing to say. (6) However, just because they said something stupid does not answer whether the Gifts are for today or not. It just means these guys allowed their head to get in the way and came up with some wacky theology. John did say Benny Hinn recanted his statements (Praise God for that), but again, that does not prove whether the Gifts operate today or not.

What John is very good at is, being very lawyer-like in assassinating the character of these men and women (an ad hominem argument), which, as we know, makes it difficult for any "jury" to believe the miracles which are actually happening. By jury I mean, you, the reader of John's books. If John can get you to mistrust the character of these people, it makes it easier for you NOT to believe the Gifts CAN operate through them. This is what politicians do nowadays (which they seldom did in years gone by) trying to bring skeletons out of the closet against their competitors so the public (jury) doesn't trust what the person is saying.

In-as-much as there is truth to the allegations made by John concerning things these people have said and done, and also towards their character, (and no we shouldn't vote into office someone without character), that can be a double edged sword. Jesus said to "Take the plank out of your eye, then you will see clearly to remove the speck from your brother's eye" (Luke 6:42). By the way, God the Holy Spirit gives out Gifts to whom He wants. Last I checked, He doesn't ask if we approve of them or not.

We are told to approve of men when it comes to leadership roles in the church, especially Pastors, Elders, and Deacons, as it pertains to character (by the way, God gives those gifts to whom he wants also; see Eph 4:11 f.f., and as Paul told Timothy and Titus, they must pass the character test before laying hands on them for these positions). But the Holy Spirit and He alone, gives His Gifts to whom He wants (1 Cor 12:11). In John's CD #137, he asks the rhetorical question, "Why would God validate His gifts through someone like Benny Hinn whose life is all messed up"?

Again, the same question can be asked of the Corinthian church; Why would God give His precious gifts to men and women at Corinth who were steeped in sin, who were divisive, carnal and sinful. I mean, who would do that? Remember what I said about Samson earlier? He was a fornicator, yet one of the most powerful men of the Spirit in the Old Testament. Those things are left to God.

But the question isn't whether or not these people are worthy of possessing the Gifts, but rather are the Gifts genuine? Who are we to question God about whom He gives what? As I stated earlier, if unbelievers wanted to give a list of phony preachers or Pastors who have fallen morally or mishandled the church's funds, they surely could. And it would probably be quite an extensive list to say the least.

If they were trying to make a point that all preachers are charlatans and liars, that we only do it for the money, or we preach it but don't live it, they most certainly could make that point. But would that be fair or accurate to the rest of us pastors who are endeavoring to live right and handle ourselves with complete integrity? I think not.

But that is what John has done to all Charismatics. He includes Charismatics. Again, not only is he saying no one truly has these Gifts today, as is proved by the way they live and the things they do, he is first and foremost saying the Gifts don't even exist today, and as to the Gifts that do exist, he redefines their functions. I cannot agree with him.

THE ONE SCRIPTURE ON WHICH HE BUILDS HIS ARGUMENT

Cessationist build their argument on one single scripture in the very book in the Bible which tells us about the Gifts and also their function, the book of 1 Corinthians.

Listen to what Dr. MacArthur says on page 360 of his 1 Corinthians commentary; *"The last miracle recorded in the New Testament in which God worked directly through a human instrument occurred about the year 58 a.d. (Acts 28:8). From that time until about 96 A.D., when John completed the writing of Revelation, not a single miracle of that sort is mentioned."*

I have to be honest with you, which is a **WEAK ARGUMENT**, if we can even call it an argument! Let me tell you why: The book of Acts is a narration of historical facts which Luke was conveying to Theophilus, as I have already stated. He was telling Theophilus the way the church functioned, and was to continue functioning. The rest of the letters in the New Testament were correcting or commending the churches on their behaviors and doctrines. And, as I also stated earlier in this book, miracles were operating in the Galatian churches, and in the Corinthian church and the Holy Spirit was present with power in the church in Thessalonica too.

In addition to that, are we really supposed to believe that miracles stopped in 58 A.D.? The Apostles were still alive after that. Peter and Paul themselves didn't die until well after that, sometime between 64-68 A.D. Other apostles lived longer than this. John most likely didn't die until about 95 a.d. Are we really to think they ceased operating in the power of the Holy Spirit just because Dr. MacArthur gives us a specious argument that they did? I think not.

Paul, in the rest of his letters in the New Testament wasn't writing to the churches to tell us, the readers, of

184

historical healings and miracles. In other words, he wasn't writing a recap of historical things like in the book of Acts. He was correcting and/or commending the churches. If we use Dr. MacArthur's logic on other church issues the same way he does on miracles and healings, the only time and the last time we hear about communion is in 1st Corinthians 11. Does that mean they stopped partaking of communion after that too? No one would agree with that logic.

So what is the verse which John and others use to make their case that the Gifts have ended?   1 Corinthians 13: 8-12.

In these five verses Paul makes clear there is coming a day when tongues, prophecy, and knowledge will be done away with. What has caused so much confusion is "when" that day is coming, and what it is that's coming. Paul says in verses 9-10, "For we know in part and we prophesy in part, but **when perfection comes**, what is in part disappears." But the question of the when and the perfect seems to be the problem.

The two main views of what perfection (or completeness) is, have been:
1) the completion of the Bible   2) second coming of Christ.

Now, for Dr.MacArthur, he does not argue for the ceasing of the Gifts in this passage as others do, to his credit. However, his argument that Paul uses different words for ceasing and stopping of the Gift of Tongues and Prophecy is no stronger than the other Cessationists concerning that which is perfect. If we hold to John's view that Prophecies will "cease" and Tongues will be "stilled," as different times of stopping, due to Paul using different words in Greek, we now have read something into the text (eisegesis) that simply is not there.

Paul made it clear: "When that which is perfect has come." Paul was telling us "when" the Gifts would come to an end, when the END COMES! The end of what? The end of this age and when the eternal age begins.

The Greek word for perfect is *teleion*. Because it is neuter in Greek, it eliminates the possibility that it relates to a person. **Keep in mind, however, Paul's point; the Gifts are imperfect until that which is perfect comes, then there will be no more need for the imperfect (Gifts). By the way, did you notice that the Gifts are imperfect?**

But please remember, there will still be Knowledge and Prophecy during the tribulation, which is BEFORE the eternal age, where God will raise up two prophetic witnesses who "will prophesy for twelve hundred and sixty days, clothed in sackcloth" (Rev

11:3). This means that Prophecy will still be in operation all the way up and through the tribulation.

If the word "perfection" means the completion of the Bible as being "that which is perfect," that would mean that Prophecy, Knowledge and Tongues would have ceased in the 1st century. However, not even Dr. MacArthur agrees with this view. The view "When the Bible is completed" honestly doesn't make any sense in the context of what Paul is saying. Let me explain why.

Even though the last book of the New Testament, the book of Revelation, was completed sometime between 90-95 a.d. The compiling of all 27 books of the New Testament wasn't done for a few hundred more years. Athanasius officially listed the 27 books in the year 367 a.d. What does that mean? That most of Christianity didn't know of or agree on which books were the official books of the Bible. In addition, even though the last book, Revelation, was completed about 95 a.d. it took many years to circulate all the New Testament letters into the hands of the churches. That means the "perfect" of which Paul speaks in 1 Corinthians 13 as being the end of the Gifts of the Spirit, couldn't be the completion of the canon of scripture as the "timeline.".

Neither does MacArthur hold to the second coming of Christ view, or of the rapture view, as the meaning of that which is perfect. (Some people don't believe in a rapture theology). Even if he did hold to either of these two views, at least they would make more sense than the view of the **Bible** being that which is "perfect." But even then, the Rapture view and the Second Coming view have not yet happened. Jesus has not yet returned. All of this means that according to the Bible itself, the Gifts are still in operation, or at least should be. When you add to that all the genuine people who have and are still operating in the Gifts, and the verified testimonies, you are now at a loss to prove the Gifts have ended.

Now, I agree with John MacArthur on his view of "**when**." He believes the "when" is the start of the eternal order. He doesn't hold to the Rapture or the Second Coming views because the eternal order doesn't begin until AFTER the Second Coming of Christ!

The Reason is, again, there are Prophecy and Knowledge going forth during the tribulation period which is to happen before the eternal, kingdom age. Dr. MacArthur states on page 365 of the same commentary, *"By process of elimination, the only possibility for **the perfect** is the eternal, heavenly state of believers."*

Let me explain:

Paul's whole argument in Chapter 13 of 1 Corinthians is, the lasting power of love over against the temporal working of the Gifts of the Spirit. On this, I agree with

John completely. Where we differ is, that somehow Dr. MacArthur believes that certain Gifts (Tongues, Interpretation of Tongues, Miracles and Healings) have already stopped or ceased when the New Testament was completed because, according to him, they were only temporary sign Gifts given to the church. On the same CD I quoted from Dr. MacArthur earlier he says, "All you have to do is look at when the these Gifts ceased to function early in Christian history to know that they are no longer in operation today." **I object!** That is an argument from experience (or the lack thereof), not an argument from scripture.

And this is where his whole argument stands on shifting sand. He has no scriptural basis for this belief. We understand that when we enter the eternal age there will be no more need for the Gifts of the Spirit, or even for the Bible itself. *"For now we see in a mirror dimly; but then face to face; now I know in part, but then I shall know fully just as I have been fully known"* (vs. 12).

In other words, in the eternal age, everything will be fully made known to us. Now we are finite beings with built-in limitations concerning The Father, Jesus, The Holy Spirit, and the why and how of things here on earth. That is why we need the Gifts of the Holy Spirit now!

But when God makes a new heaven and a new earth, we will forever be with the Lord. There won't be any sickness or disease, death or crying, pain, or darkness. We will have no need of Bible study to know how God wants us to live, or what to believe. We won't need knowledge of what to do next, or Prophecy to tell us what is yet to come.

As John says in Revelation 21:22-25, "I did not see a temple in the city, because the Lord God almighty and the Lamb are its temple. The city does not need the sun or the moon to shine on it, for the glory of God gives it light, and the Lamb is its lamp. The nations will walk by its light, and the kings of the earth will bring their splendor into it. On no day will its gates ever be shut, for there will be no night there."

Where Dr. MacArthur and I disagree is, he randomly picks Tongues, Interpretation of Tongues, Miracles and Healings as Gifts that simply disappeared from the church during the early church age, discarding all the proof from history that these Gifts are still alive and well all over the world and are still being utilized by Born Again Charismatic Christians who are not phony or goofy or only in it for the money!

If the Bible doesn't say the Gifts were only for the first century and nowhere does it say that four out of the nine Gifts would stop (per MacArthur), and if Christians have and are still operating in them as proof they still exist, then you have a dilemma on your hands. You either will simply hold on to what you have always been taught, or you will be honest with yourself that the Bible does not support what you thought was true about the Gifts ceasing, and you will now change your view and your prayers.

John offers no Biblical proof that they have stopped. In fact, the Word of God states just the opposite. Look at Mark 16:15-18, *"He said to them, Go into all the world and preach the good news to all creation. Whoever believes and is baptized will be saved, but whoever does not believe will be condemned. And these signs shall accompany those who believe: In my name they shall drive out demons; they will speak in new tongues; they will pick up snakes with their hands; and when they drink deadly poison, it will not hurt them at all; they will place their hands on sick people, and they will get well."*

I know this passage found in Mark's gospel wasn't found in the earliest and most reliable manuscripts, but because the theology contained in it lines up with the rest of New Testament theology, it remained part of scripture until this present day. It agrees with with what we know to be true about Christianity as a whole

Do you see now? The Gifts for the church are for the church age, which we are still in. The Gifts are manifestations of God's Spirit given out to each one as the Spirit determines. The purpose is to build up the body of Christ through their proper use. There is to be order and structure to their functioning. Everything is to be judged as to its accuracy and authenticity. Never should there be any phony manifestations or unsound doctrines taking place in our Christian churches.

But neither should there be a quenching of the Spirit in our assembly times. I remind you again of what Paul said, *"Do not quench the Holy Spirit, and do not treat prophecies with contempt. And again, "Therefore, my brothers, be eager to prophesy, and do not forbid speaking in tongues. But everything should be done in a fitting and orderly way."*

CHAPTER 14

AIMEE SEMPLE MCPHERSON

Who was Aimee Semple Mcpherson?

Aimee Semple Mcpherson was the founder of the Foursquare denomination known as the International Church of the Foursquare Gospel, or, ICFG. Let me give you a little of her background. This is a much truncated version of the whole story of her life, but I will give you some highlights. Much, much more could be said, but that is not the purpose of this book. If you want to read the full and detailed account of her life, go to the Foursquare website and look up some of her books. A good one to start is called, "Aimee, My Personal Story." You will not be disappointed.

In the late 1880's, in Toronto Canada, there was a man by the name of James Kennedy. His wife was deathly sick, so he put an ad in the newspaper for "in-home" care (something like hospice care today). A young lady answered the ad and came and took care of Mrs. Kennedy as she was dying. Unfortunately, after a short time, Mrs. Kennedy did pass away.

Mr. Kennedy had grown fond of this young lady who had so graciously and lovingly taken care of his wife, and he fell in love with her. Her name was Mildred, but she was called "Minnie" for short. Mr. Kennedy proposed to her and she agreed to be his wife now that his wife had died. There was just one catch; James was 50 and Minnie was 15!

As you can imagine, talk quickly went around the town of what was taking place, but James and Minnie were madly in love, so marry they did. About a year and half later their only child, a daughter named Aimee was born. The year was 1890.

Her mother Minnie was a devout and God fearing woman who had wanted to be used for God's glory herself, but would now do that vicariously through her beautiful daughter Aimee. When Minnie was pregnant with Aimee, she would place her own hands on her swollen belly and ask God to bless this child in her womb and use her mightily for Him. God was going to do this in the most dramatic way.

Aimee, being an only child, was quite creative and self amusing. Her mom read Bible stories to her every night and would try to do that in a very "story-telling" type of way. Aimee was enthralled with her mother's ability to make the stories in the Bible come alive. Needless to say, Aimee became quite the little actress from an early age.

As Aimee made her way through school, she would often be in the school plays and frequently had the lead role. She was very talented at public speaking and won competitions throughout her junior high and high school years. But one thing bothered her as she was in high school; the things she read in the Bible about miracles and healings weren't being done in the churches she knew and had attended. One day she decided to ask her pastor why they didn't see miracles anymore like in the Bible, and the answer he gave her was so pathetic, "those things don't happen in our day," that she decided to become an atheist.

Aimee's father wasn't too pleased with her decision. One night as he and his now "atheist daughter" were riding the buggy into town, they saw a sign which said, "Week long revival with evangelist Robert Semple." Aimee's dad told her that he was taking her to the revival. Aimee went, kicking and screaming all the way, but dad would not budge. So, that night they went to the tent meeting and sat in the back. The year was 1908.

After the music and the singing, out onto the platform came the evangelist. He was nothing like Aimee imagined him to be. She was expecting a balding pot-bellied man in his 60's. But Robert was far from that. He was 6'2," with wavy brown hair and deep blue eyes. Aimee was star struck. She was mesmerized by his striking good looks and his powerful preacher's voice.

As Robert Semple began to preach on the love of Jesus and the power of the Holy Spirit, and how God wanted to fill every believer with this precious gift, a new fire and hunger began to burn in her soul. By the time Robert was done preaching, Aimee was repenting of her sin and backslidings and was desperately asking God to fill her with the Holy Spirit, with the evidence of speaking in other tongues.

 The Azusa street outpourings had begun just a couple of years before this encounter of Robert and Aimee, and Robert had been greatly influenced by the revival of "glossalalia," or what is more commonly known as Tongues. This would have a major impact and effect on Aimee's life and story.

Aimee began to tarry, or seek, the Lord desperately for this precious gift of the Holy Spirit.

Tongues was the long-lost blessing of the church which God was pouring out again as the "latter rain," so it was being said. It had been absent, or at least marginalized by the church for centuries except in small pockets, or held by those who would be called heretics at best. But Aimee believed what she had seen and heard from Robert and it totally lined up with scripture in the book of Acts and 1 Corinthians. After tarrying (waiting) for some time to be filled by God, one morning after much prayer, it happened. She began to speak in the most beautiful language as it came bubbling out of her belly, just as John's gospel said it would (John 7:37-39).

Right after this, Robert proposed to Aimee who, with much excitement and a deep love, said "Yes." A few weeks later they were married and began their life together. Aimee said she was deeply in love and thoroughly enjoyed traveling with her husband as he continued his ministry as an itinerant evangelist. She played the piano and Robert preached.

As Aimee tells the story, Robert became her Bible college professor. She was his private and only student. She grew deeper in love with her husband and came to know her Bible very well. Of course, God had gifted and trained her since she was a little girl with all the contests she won and the plays she starred in, to one day become a great speaker for Him. The Gifts would not go unused as far as God was concerned.

A CRISIS HITS THEIR LIVES

Robert felt the call to go to China to be a missionary. His new wife wasn't so sure. But after much prayer and convincing, the two agreed it was the Lord's will for them to go. So off to China they went. Aimee was heavy with child.

After being there a short while in deplorable living conditions, Robert became deathly ill from eating some garden vegetables which had been fertilized with human excrement. Even though Aimee prayed and believed feverishly for his healing, it wasn't meant to be. Robert died in China after just a couple months of being there, leaving Aimee a widow and eight months pregnant! Tough times lay ahead for her.

Her mother, Minnie, eventually got her back to the United States and Aimee and her new little daughter Roberta, moved in with her mom. It was a very difficult time for Aimee. The grief from the loss of her husband and their ministry plans and dreams were almost too much to bear. She went through a time of depression, but God gave her grace and strength to bear up under it.

She began to call on some of the pastors and churches which had allowed her husband Robert to preach at their churches, but with only little success. After not being used much for a time, she felt God was calling her to preach His gospel. By now she met and had fallen in love with a man by the name of Harold McPherson.

He was a businessman and didn't feel the call to the ministry. He wanted Aimee to be a stay-at-home wife and mother. She now was pregnant with her second child, a boy named Rolf. He would later become the leader of the Foursquare denomination which his mother had started. After Rolf was born Aimee began to feel restless concerning ministry. She would pray and ask God to show her what to do, and that if God didn't want her to preach, why did He put such a burden in heart to do so?

Finally she couldn't take it anymore, and began going out to the street corners, preaching and passing out flyers, talking to anyone who would listen. Because she was so theatrical, crowds would gather to hear what this unusual and peculiar lady had to say. The crowds kept growing.

Once, after preaching in a church where they took up an offering for her, she got enough money to buy a used tent. When she opened it up, it was so badly torn that she and a couple of helpers spent two days hand-stitching it to get it ready for a tent meeting.

Unfortunately, her husband Harold McPherson didn't want any part of this women preacher thing. But one night at a tent meeting revival she was conducting, she collected enough money to buy a Packard car. She begged her husband to come and join her, and for a while, he did. He would drive and Aimee would stand on the back seat with a megaphone and preach the gospel and invite people to their evening revivals. The crowds kept growing and more and more people were repenting of their sins and giving their lives to Jesus Christ.

THE GIFTS OF HEALINGS BEGIN

As she continued growing in popularity, becoming
more and more powerful in her preaching and more
creative in her proclamation of the gospel, one night a
lady came down at the end of service at Aimee's call
for the sick to and be prayed for. She came from the
back of the tent and approached the altar where Aimee
was. When Aimee looked up and saw her, she gasped
at the lady's appearance. She was crippled with her
neck sharply tilted to one side and not a little
deformed. Aimee thought to herself, "Dear Lord, what
can I possibly do for this lady?" But with all the faith
she had, she prayed for the woman to be healed in
Jesus name. In front of the entire congregation, and to
Aimee's utter amazement, the woman straightened up
and was instantly and completely healed! Little did
Aimee know that this would begin a worldwide
healing ministry. Once news of this miracle began to
spread there was no stopping the crowds.

BELOW IS A TRANSCRIPT OF A MESSAGE WHICH WAS PREACHED BY AIMEE SEMPLE MCPHERSON CONCERNING THE DAMAGE CESSATIONIST THEOLOGY HAS DONE TO THE BODY OF CHRIST

Is Jesus Christ The Great "I AM" or Is He The Great "I Was?"

A sermon of a dream about Cessationist theology and why churches are empty.

Shut in my closet of prayer today, with my Bible and the Spirit, my Guide, I muse a while o'er its pages, then pray for the world with its throngs who, in teeming millions, walk through this life in need of 'The Great I AM."

As I ponder and pray in the stillness, I dream as a dreamer of dreams, A steepled church stands before me a church with open doors. Within it I see the preacher stand; hear his voice in earnest call. But 'tis the throng that flows through the street outside that holds my anxious gaze.

"Pit-a-pat! Pit-a-pat!" say the hundreds and thousands of feet, surging by the church doors of our land. "Pat! Pat! Pit-a-pat!" hurrying multitudes, on business and

202

pleasure bent. From out the church door floats the voice of Pastor and Evangelist in an effort to halt the down-rushing throng in their headlong race toward destruction and attract their attention to the Christ.

"Stop! Stop! Giddy throng, surging by like a river, take your eyes from the bright lights of the gilded way," they cry. "Leave the paths of death, enter our open door and listen while we tell you the sweet though ancient story of 'The Great I WAS.'

"Eloquently, instructively, we will tell you of the wonderful power Christ 'used' to have, the miracles He 'used' to perform, the sick He 'used' to heal. 'Tis a graphic and blessed history of those things which Jesus did almost 1900 years before you were born. They happened far, far away from across a sea which you have never sailed, in a country which you have never seen, among people you have never known.

"Wonderful, marvelous, was the power that 'used' to flow from 'The Great I WAS.' He 'used' to open the blind eyes, unstop the deaf ears, and make the lame to walk. He 'used' to show forth such mighty works, and even manifest them through His followers that the attention of the multitudes was arrested and gripped in such an irresistible way that thousands were brought storming at His door of mercy, to receive blessing and healing at His hand.

'Of course, these mighty works Christ 'used' to do are done no longer, for some reason. Perhaps Jesus is too far away, or is too busy making intercession at the Father's throne to be bothered with such little things as the physical infirmities of His children, else.

His ear may have grown heavy or His arm be short, or maybe these mighty works were only done to convince the doubters in that day, and since we have no doubters (?) in this civilized day and age, the miraculous has passed away and is no longer necessary.

"Come, come to this attractive feast, unheeding sinners. Turn now from Sunday golf (emphasis added MD), fishing, theatres and novels! Come enter our doors that I may tell you the story of ' The Great I WAS.' and the power that 'used' to be."

But "Pit-a-pat! Pit-a-pat!" On go the thousands of feet; on to the movie and on to the dance; and on to the office, the club and the bank.

"Pat! Pat! Pit-a-Pat!" "Why don't you stop your wayward feet? Do, you not know that you are headed for sorrow? Why is it that the theatre is o'er flowing whilst our pews are empty and bare?"

"Pat! Pat! Pat! Pit-a-pat!" "Oh stop a moment, the maddening, ceaseless, pattering of multitudinous feet and tell me why you take such an interest in the world about you and show such lethargy, carelessness and lack of active interest in my story 'The Great I WAS/

and the power He 'used' to have and the deeds He 'used' to do? Why is it that people grow enthusiastic over the ball-game, the boxing ring, the movies and the dance, while we see no revival of interest or turning to the Christ?"

On and on they go paying no heed, neither turning their eyes from the glittering baubles beyond. "Why is it, dear Spirit of God," I ask, they do not listen to the dear Brother's call? They do not seem interested in the power Christ 'used' to have. In a steady stream they pass by the church and on into the world of grim realities and the problems which they must face.

"Pat! Pat! Pit-a-pat!" 'there are young feet, old feet, light feet, heavy feet, glad feet, sad feet; joyous feet, tired discouraged feet, tripping feet; lonely, groping feet; straight feet, sick and crippled feet; eager, searching feet; disillusioned, disappointed feet; and, as they pass, a message is somehow tangled up in their pattering, which rises from the cobble-stones like a mighty throbbing from the heart of the world.

" 'Tis not so much what Christ used to do for the world in answer to prayer in bygone days," they seem to say, "but where is His power NOW? And what can He do TODAY?" "Ah yes!", sigh the crippled feet from the pavement, "we are not so vitally interested in the sick He 'used' to heal, the limbs He 'used' to make straight and strong.

(Of course, we are glad to know that somewhere, sometimes, in the distant past Christ healed the sick in far off lands). But we live in the great today and Ah me! ! We are very worn and weary! We yearn for healing, hope and strength today. We stand in need of succor NOW. But you say these mighty provisions for the healing of the body, (as well as the soul), which Christ promised in Psalms 103, Isaiah 53; Matt. 8; Mark 16; Jas 5; were not at all lasting, but were mainly for the Jews who lived in other days. And in reality your teaching says Christ's healing of the sick, when He walked this earth, was not so much for the demonstration of the tender Savior's love and sake of relieving the sufferer's pain and a pity for the sick themselves, as to build up His own cause and make the world believe and accomplishing this, He withdrew the life line of hope and coiled it up again. So, as the church cannot supply my need, I must pass on in further search of help from another source."

"And we," say the tired, discouraged feet, "are also glad that in a far off land, He gave the weary rest; and they, who had well nigh lost the faith and trust in their fellow-man, found truth and grace in Him. "But you say He is afar off now? That we live in a different dispensation? His promises were largely for the Jewish people anyway? Then there's not much for us here, so we walk past your door seeking elsewhere a haven of rest and hope."

"And we," the glad, young, joyous feet, send up a rippling echo from the pavement, "we are in search of something that can give us joy and happiness today. You say God 'used' to make His little ones so happy

206

that they danced and shouted for joy. We, too, want joy! Not the joy that 'used' to be but joy of heart today. As it is taken away from the church, we seek it in the world."

"And we, say the heavy, groping, loney feet," are bereaved and seek comfort and rest. For us the shades of night are falling. The knowledge that Christ 'once' dried tears and bare the heavy load is blest indeed, but Oh!, we of today need succor now, Preaching 'The Great I WAS' can never satisfy our longings, WE NEED 'THE GREAT I AM.'

"The Great I AM" why yes! That's it exactly!

That's what this old world needs. A Christ who lives and loves and answers prayer today. *A Christ who changeth not but is the same today as He was yesterday, and will be evermore.* A Christ whose power knows neither ack nor cessation. A Lord whose Name is "I AM" forever, even unto all generations.

When the Lord bade Moses go, call the children of Israel from the flesh pots and bondage, sin and sickness of Egypt, Moses inquired of Him, "When they shall ask who sent me? And What is His Name? What shall I say unto them?" and He said, "Thus shalt thou say unto the children of Israel, I AM hath sent me unto you. This is my Name forever, and this is memorial unto all generations."

Oh, what a wonderful Name! What a wonderful promise! Glory! Glory! to God!

Moses did not need to go about apologetically and say, 'The Great I WAS' hath sent me unto you, His name is 'I WAS' because He 'used' to do great things long ago. He expended the last of His power in creating the heavens and the earth and all that in them is. He is quite far off now and the necessity for this miraculous manifestation of His power is no longer needed, seeing that all things have now been created. He does not do mighty works today but please come, follow and obey the message of 'The Great I WAS.'

Why I doubt whether they would have followed such a call. The message which Moses bore rang clear and firm "I AM hath sent me." He walked with assurance. The solid rock was under his feet.

His God was a living God a miracle-working God. Moses knew his business was to preach and deliver the message God had given him. "The Great I AM" had contracted to back up that message with signs following. "I AM I AM I AM!" rang in the ears of Moses every step he took.

Ah! It gives a servant of God some heart to know that "I AM" hath sent him.

No more apologizing. No more hanging the head and resorting to earthy means; no more trembling and fear of failure, no dread now that the crowds will not follow! Head erect, footsteps firm and full of assurance, earthly temple clad with a robe of the majesty and tenderness of the Father, hands pointing unhesitatingly to the way, voice ringing clear and authoritative "I AM, I AM hath sent me unto you!"

Oh, the blessed assurance, the authority, the majestic glory of the name "I AM!" No wonder the children of Israel left the flesh-pots and the bands that bound them. No wonder the weary eyes of the toiler looked up with new interest and hope. No wonder that hdns which had hung down were lifted and the feeble knees made strong when Moses could promise them that when the Lord said unto those which were weak, "Be strong and of good courage, for the Lord will do great things, "He meant just what He said.

He did not have to say, "The Lord 'used' to do great things," but could triumphantly declare, "The Lord 'will' do great things; for He is 'The Great I AM', and though heaven is His home, the earth is His footstool where He answers the prayers of His people."

During Moses' ministry, the sick were healed, the lepers cleansed, the plague stayed. Oh Moses how we envy you, the great commission, GO! call my people out of bondage into liberty; out of darkness into light; out of sin into holiness; out of sickness into health! But tell us, just when did he day of supernatural, miraculous manifestation of the power of God end? When did "I AM" become "I WAS?"

On and on through the centuries, though surrounded by unbelief and skepticism; there have always been the Elijahs and the Peters who have proved that "I AM" is His Name even unto their generation. John Wesley believed that Christ was not only to save but to heal the sick in his day. In his biography he tells of the lame made to walk, cancers which melted away and even a lame horse made whole through answered prayer; thus proving "I AM" to be the Lord's Name even unto his generation. Then surely He has not changed at this late hour! Surely, He is the same today.

Elijah, Peter, John Wesley and an army of others who had heard and obeyed the message, "Thus shall you say I AM hath sent me were ridiculed and persecuted by those they loved the best. Even so today, though it means being despised and misunderstood, get alone in the wilderness of quiet and stillness before God. Seek His face till your soul is kindled with the flame of love from the burning bush. Get your authority from God. Inquire of Him, "When they shall ask who sent me and what is His name, what shall I say unto them?" Hear His reply," Thus shalt thou say unto them, 'I AM' hath sent me" and let it ring in your soul forever, louder, clearer, more wonderful in its revelation of the ever-living Christ with each new step and turn of the way.

Victory is assured and the only solution to the problem of drawing the multitude is to lift up, not the dead, but the living Christ; not the Great "I WAS" but the Great "I AM."

The clouds of uncertainty are dispelled the shades of night rolled back. We, see Thee in a new and glorious light, even as the Sun of Righteousness with healing in

Thy wings, "I AM" is Thy Name today and shall be evermore!

"I AM the Lord, I change not."

"I AM the Lord that hath chosen thee and called thee by thy name."

"I AM come down to deliver thee and to bring thee up into a good land and a large; unto a land flowing with milk and honey."

"I AM (not I WAS but I AM) the Lord that healeth thee."

"I AM He who was dead but am alive forevermore."

"I AM Alpha and Omega, the beginning and the end, the first and the last."

Again, I see the steepled church, but now the scene is changed.

"Pat! Pat! Pit-a-pat" - The street that lies before it is still with people filled, But they are no longer passing "by"- The crowds are passing "in."

They fill the pews and the galleries. They stand in the aisles and climb to the window sills. They pack the doorways and stand on the stairs. The streets and the

211

lanes are filled. The Gospel nets are full to the bursting and there is no more room to contain the multitudes that throng the place.

And out o'er the heads of the people I hear the message ring:

'Awake! Thou that sleepest, arise-from the dead!

The Lord still lives today. His power has never abated. His Word has never changed. The things

He did in Bible Days, He still lives to do today, Not a burden is there He cannot bear nor a fetter

He cannot break.

"Here bring your sicknesses He'll heal you today. We serve not a dead but a living God, not 'I

WAS,' but 'The Great I Am.'

"Come young, come old; come sad, come glad; come weary and faltering of step; come sick, come well! Come one, come all unto I The Great I AM.' There is food for the hungry, there is strength for the faint; there is hope for the hopeless, and sight for the blind."

'Pit-a-pat! Pit-a-pat!" Faster and faster they come! The church is o'erflowing; they are filling the streets. Their faces are shining; in their eyes the light of hope has been kindled by the taper of faith through the preaching of "The Great I AM."

They are reaching out their hands for forgiveness, for the healing of the crippled and sick. They are thirsting for the joy of salvation; hungering for the Bread of Life. They are seeking the power of the Holy Ghost and something practical which can meet the immediate and pressing need of the great today, and fit them for the morrow. And they have found the source of sure supply in the church the house of God from under whose altar and o'er whose threshold runs the ever deepening stream of life. They seek no further, through the briers of the world they have found "The Great I AM."

"Wisdom, righteousness and power,

Holiness forevermore

My redemption full and sure,

Christ is all I need."

Burdens are lifted, tearful weeping eyes are dried, the sick are healed, the crooked made straight. Sin-guilty hearts are cleansed and made holy. Empty water-pots are filled with wine. And the cold, worldly church has risen from the dust in garments glistering, white. With oil in their lamps and sheaves in their arms they worship "The Great I AM."

CHAPTER 15

TO ALL MY CESSATIONIST BROTHERS AND SISTERS

Some loving words from my heart to yours

As a brother in our Lord and Savior Jesus Christ, and one who preaches the gospel as a way of life, I want to encourage you in your faith, or as Paul says, "That you and I might mutually be encouraged by each other's faith" (Romans 1:12).

First let me define the gospel which I preach:

Jesus Christ was God before the manger

He was born of a virgin

He lived a sinless life

He died on the cross

His blood paid for the sins of the whole world

He was buried dead

He bodily rose from the grave by the power of God

He appeared to over 500 people

He gave last instructions to the apostles

He ascended to Heaven

He is seated at the right hand of God in authority

He is coming back one day as King of kings, and Lord of lords

He is the way, the truth, and the life. No man comes to the Father except through Him

We are saved by grace through faith in Christ alone

If you believe in your heart that God raised Him from the dead and confess with your mouth that Jesus is Lord, you shall be saved

This is what I believe and what I preach. I hope that you believe ALL these things as well. For if you untie ONE of them, you untie them all.

Trusting that you do believe all these biblical truths about Jesus, when you began this book you may have been a Cessationist (and you still might be). If you are still a Cessationist, or maybe you are unsure, I want you to know that you are still my brothers and sisters in the Lord. One day I will see you in heaven, if we never get to meet on this side of glory. Our differences in theology concerning tongues and the gifts will not separate us now, or in eternity. And that includes my dear friend and mentor in the faith, John MacArthur.

My desire was to bring you to a fuller understanding of the truths of scripture in order that your life and ministry might flow with more of His power and authority. There will always be sick and diseased people among us, those who are discouraged and beaten down by life, the devil, and their own decisions which hurt their lives. Our job in the body of Christ is to minister to them with great love and acceptance, and offer them something that goes beyond human ingenuity, wisdom, and even at times, medicine.

Ours is a sin-sick world, where the prince of the power of the air is still at work in the children of disobedience (Eph 2:2). But we have something greater within us then he that is in the world   (1 John 4:4). "His divine power power has given us everything we need for life and godliness through our knowledge of him who called us by his own glory and goodness" (2 Peter 1:3). That power is from the Holy Spirit who dwells in each believer. As Jesus said, "You shall receive power when the Holy Spirit comes on you..." (Acts 1:8).

It is the precious Gifts of the Holy Spirit that I am trying to encourage you to seek after   (1 Corinthians 14:1). It is only in His power that we are able to minister in another dimension. It is still ours today, and it will continue to be until Jesus returns and makes all things new. Then, and only then will there be no more pain, sorrow, sickness, or death (Revelation 21:4). But for now, we have to deal with these earthly problems brought on by sin and the enemy of our souls.

Thank God for His grace, power, and goodness which have been given to us who believe. As Jesus told the disciples, "Heal the sick who are there and tell them, 'The kingdom of God is near you'" (Luke 10:9).

SUMMARIZING THE GIFTS

In summary, nowhere does the Bible say the Gifts have ceased after the Apostles, or after the first century, or after the completion of the New Testament. The Gifts have been in operation all throughout Christian history with a great resurgence over the last century in many godly men and women.

There are multiple thousands of testimonies around the globe, including here in the United States, of people who have and are operating in these Gifts, and many verified reports. I have personally operated in them, and fellow ministers I know, such as Mario Murillo, still do, and have medically documented healings and miracles which can and have been verified.

SUMMARIZING TONGUES

Tongues have a purpose when shared in the local congregation but only when followed by the Gift of Interpretation. These two together are for the building up of the body of Christ and are equal to Prophecy in their effect. Private tongues, or a prayer language, is for building up the individual and for speaking mysteries, praise, and thanksgiving.

Tongues in Acts and Corinthians had, and have, two different purposes, and confusion will come if you do not separate them. Tongues may be in a human language or in a heavenly language. Just because you don't understand what is being spoken does not mean they are bizarre or gibberish.

Lastly, we are commanded to "not quench" the Holy Spirit and to not forbid prophesying or speaking in tongues, but everything must be done in a fitting and orderly way. All the Gifts are given for building up the body of Christ and will remain in operation until the eternal order is established, after the second coming of Christ.

In conclusion

It is my hope and prayer that each of you who read this book will go after the things of the Spirit and step out in the supernatural. Ask God about these things. Read the Word of God over and over and look for the truths contained in it. Talk to your Pastors about them and have them read this book and then set up an appointment to talk openly with them about the things you have read. This book is meant to be irenic, not divisive.

Concerning John MacArthur and me, no need to worry about us. We have another golf date planned and by the time you read this, we will have been talking and laughing and discussing more theology, until Jesus returns or takes us home. I love John. He loves me. I am the token Charismatic in his group. And you know everybody has to have one of those. And just so you know, when John is with me and my friends, he is the **Token Cessationist!**

Blessings on you all,

Pastor Gary

The Token Charismatic

Chapter 1
1 Corinthians 11:19, The New International
Version
Romans 14:1
Walter Martin ministries; Resource Catalog, CD
Entitled 'Gifts of the Holy Spirit' #3022
James 3:1
2 Timothy 2:15
1 Peter 3:15
1 Corinthians 12-14
Tedford, The Letters of John Wesley, nd. 2:261

Chapter 2
Hebrews 13:8
Acts 14:8-10
Acts 17:11
Acts 19:24-26
Acts 13:2
Acts 14:8
John 6:44, 65
Luke 10:20
Acts 10:38
Acts 1:1
1 John 3:8
Matthew 4:23-24
Acts 16:1-3
2 Timothy 1:13
2 Timothy 2:1-2

Acts 14:8-10
Dr. J.Vernon McGee, "Speaking in Tongues",
Pages 14-15
Luke 13:10-13
1 Corinthians 8:1
1 Timothy 4:13

Chapter 3
Acts 1:8
Acts 3:12
James 5:14
1 Corinthians 12:7-10
Dr. Jack Hayford and Dr. David Moore, The
Charismatic Century
1 Corinthians 14:1
Psalms 78:4
Matthew 28:19-20
Luke 10:3
Luke 10:9
Acts 4:29-30
Acts 5:12-16
2 Corinthians 5:20
Acts 4:29-30
Mark 6:5

Chapter 4
Dr. John MacArthur, Strange Fire
2 Timothy 2:15
1 Thessalonians 5:21
Phil 1:15-17
Heb 10:25
Eph 4:14
John 14:12
Acts 1:4
Acts 1:8
1 Cor 12:11
1 Co 14:39-40
John MacArthur, 1 Corinthians 14 Commentary
John MacArthur, Epistle of James Commentary
Dr. Richard Mayhue, The Healing Promise
Gordon Fee, God's Empowering Presence

Chapter 5
1 Co 14:1
Romans 12:6-7
Psalm 119:89
Wayne Grudem, Systematic Theology
1 Co 14:3
John MacArthur and Phil Johnson, CD# GTY 137, dated 2012
Acts 21:9
1 Co 14
1 Thess 5:19-22
2 Co 12:12
Acts 15:32

Ephesians 2:19-20
1 Thess 5:19
Acts 21:10
2 Kings 2 and 6
Acts 11:28
1 Co 14:3
1 Co 14:1
1 Thess 5:19-21
1 Co 14:29-33
1 Co 14:18
1 Co 12:7
1 Co 1:7
Judges 14:6
Judges 14:1
Galatians 6:7
1 Co 14:1

Chapter 6
1 Co 12
1 Co 12:1, 4
1 Kings 17
2 Kings 2
1 Kings 21:17-19
1 Kings 19:16
2 Kings 2:9-10
2 Kings 4:8-28
2 Kings 5
Mark 11:1-6
Mark 14:12-16
Acts 5:1-11

Acts 2:45
Acts 4:36-37
Acts 9:11
1 Co 12
1 Co 12:8
Ephesians 1:15-19
Colossians 2:3
James 1:5
2 Sam 5:19
2 Sam 5:22-25
John MacArthur, 1 Corinthians 12 Commentary
Colossians 3:16
Matthew 17:24-27
Acts 8:4-8, 26-40

Chapter 7
Gordon Fee, God's Empowering Presence
1 Co 14:10
1 Co 13:1
John 16:13
Romans 8:26-27
John 12:49-50
John MacArthur, Romans 8 Commentary
Acts 2:1-4
Acts 19:6
Acts 2, 9, 19
Acts 8:4-8
Acts 8:13
Acts 9:17
1 Co 14:18

Acts 2:11
Acts 2
Acts 10:45
Acts 19:6
Isaiah 28:7-12
1 Co 14:5
1 Co 14:11-13, 27-28
1 Co 14:20-28
1 Co 14:1
John MacArthur, The Simple, Surprising Truth
about Tongues, CD #44-7T dated, 2014
1 Co 14:21/Isaiah 28:11,12
1 Co 12:8-10
1 Co 14:18
1 Co 14:1-17
Jude 20
Dr. Jerry Cook, his book on the Holy Spirit
Jude 20
Ephesians 6:18
1 Co 14:14
Mark 9:1-29
Acts 4:29-31
Acts 2:38
Joel 2:28
Romans 8:9
1 Co 4:16-17
John MacArthur, 1 Corinthians Commentary, CD
on the Holy Spirit and Tongues
Galatians 3:5
Acts 14:21-23; 15:36, 41; 18:23
Acts 1:4
1 Co 14:4, 7

Chapter 8
1 Co 14:13
1 Co 14:5
1 Co 14:28
1 Co 14:39

Chapter 9
John MacArthur, 1 Corinthians Commentary, pages 297-298
Tappert, ed., Luther: Letters of Spiritual Counsel, nd. 18:52, Ch.1, p.52
Dr. Walter Martin, CD #3022
Acts 4:12
Matt 9:35-37
Matt 14:14, *King James Version*
Matt 15:32
Matt 20:34
Mark 1:41, 5:19, 6:34, 8:2, 9:22
Luke 7:13
John 14:9-10
1 John 3:8
Acts 10:38, *New International Version*
Luke 4:18-19
Mark 6:1-6
John 5:1-15
Acts 3:1-10

Luke 18:8
John 5:19-20
John 10:10
Isaiah 61:1
Acts 2:38
Luke 10:9
Acts 6:8
Acts 8:5
Acts 28:8
Galatians 3:5
Romans 4:17
Acts 1:1
John 14:12
1 Co 14:1
2 Tim 4:2
Mark 16:15-18
Mark 8:22-23

Chapter 10
2 Tim 4:7
Romans 12:3
Hebrews 11:6
Phil 4:6-8
John MacArthur, 1 Corinthians 12 Commentary,
page 300
Acts 6:8, 11:24
Matt 14:22-29
Hebrews 11:1

Chapter 11
2 Co 11:13-15
Jude 4
Acts 16
Acts 16:11-15
Acts 16:16
Luke 13:16
Acts 8:4-17
Acts 20:29-30
2 Peter 2:1-3

Chapter 12
1 Co 14:32-33
1 Thess 5:19
1 Co 14:27-28, 31
1 Thess 5:21
1 Co 14:29
John MacArthur, 1 Corinthians, Romans, 1
Thessalonians Commentaries
Charismatic Chaos, John MacArthur
Eph 2:19-20
1 Co 14

Chapter 13
Luke 6:42
Eph 4:11
1 Co 12:11
John MacArthur and Phil Johnson, CD# GTY 137, dated 2012
1 Corinthians Commentary, page 360, John MacArthur
Acts 28:8
1 Co 11:27-29
1 Co 13:8-12
Rev 11:13
John MacArthur, 1 Corinthians Commentary, page 365
1 Co 13:12
Rev 21:22-25
Mark 16:15-18
1 Thess 5:19
1 Co 14:39

Chapter 14
John 7:38
Aimee Semple McPherson, Is Jesus Christ The Great "I AM" or Is He The Great "I Was?"

Chapter 15
Romans 1:12
Ephesians 2:2
1 John 4:4
Acts 1:8
1 Co 14:1
Rev 21:4
Luke 10:9

(Left to right) Pastor Gary Mortara, Matt MacArthur,
Dr. MacArthur, Friend of Dr. MacArthur

(Left to right) Pastor Gary Mortara, Dr. MacArthur,
John MacArthur (Grandson), Dr. Larry Epperson

233

(Left to right) Friend of John MacArthur, Matt
MacArthur, Dr. MacArthur, Pastor Gary Mortara

234

(left to right) Dr. MacArthur, Grandson John, Friend of
Dr. MacArthur, Pastor Gary Mortara

(Left to right) Dr. Larry Epperson , Hank Hanagraf,
Dr. MacArthur, Pastor Gary Mortara

Made in the USA
Charleston, SC
02 October 2015